Goddess Walks Beside You
How You Can Listen, Learn and Enjoy the Wiccan Path

from GoddessHasYourBack.com

Moonwater SilverClaw
Wiccan High Priestess
Blogger/Founder of
GoddessHasYourBack.com
with visitors from **173 countries**

A QuickBreakthrough Publishing Edition

More copies are available from the publisher with the imprint QuickBreakthrough Publishing. For more information about this book contact: askawitchnow@gmail.com

This book was developed and written with care. Names and details were modified to respect privacy.

Other Books by Moonwater SilverClaw:

- Goddess Has Your Back
- The Hidden Children of the Goddess
- Beyond the Law of Attraction to Real Magick

Praise for Moonwater SilverClaw:

• "In her book *The Hidden Children of the Goddess*, Moonwater brings Wicca to life, enveloping you in the mystery and magick of the Craft. Her writing talent is amazing! Her kindness and even sense of fun is ever present throughout her writing. Moonwater expresses profound Wicca concepts through examples in her own life experience. Wicca actually saved her life. and empowered her to leave an abusive marriage, and this shows the power of this sacred path to positively change the course of our lives, too. Moonwater's stories personally inspire me, and I am confident that they will inspire you also." – Rev. Patrick McCollum, internationally recognized spiritual leader working for human rights, social justice, and equality; the 2010 recipient of the Mahatma Gandhi Award for the Advancement of Pluralism.

• "Religion scholars in the future will likely view Moonwater SilverClaw as the pivotal voice that helped change the discourse on Wicca. In her book *Goddess Has Your Back,* Moonwater reveals Wicca as a very positive and ultimately uplifting spirituality choice. She demystifies the religion's taboos and spooky stereotypes through her unintimidating presentation that clarifies the topic. She introduces the Goddess and the magick rituals that, when used properly, can positively impact your everyday life. The author relays her very personal perspective on the subject and shows how to integrate the philosophies and practices of the centuries-old religion. Looking for a fresh perspective on spiritual growth? Read what Moonwater SilverClaw has to say. She may very well point you in the direction where you need to go." – Stacy D. Horn

• "Moonwater's writing will give you a portrait of a woman who lives her faith, and whose life was saved by it. Because so many lives, my own included, were irrevocably changed by Wicca, were given new focus, new purpose, and perhaps most importantly, new personal power to realize one's dreams and ambitions. . . . It's a story about making your own happy endings, about rescuing yourself, and that, I believe, is what makes writing like this necessary." – Jason Pitzl-Waters, blogger at WildHunt.org

Visit Moonwater's blog: www.GoddessHasYourBack.com

CONTENTS

DEDICATION AND ACKNOWLEDGEMENTS

This book is dedicated to the God and Goddess. Thanks to Tom Marcoux for editing. Thanks to Kay Pannell for her guidance and friendship.

CHAPTER ONE

GODDESS WALKS BESIDE YOU

Have you felt the presence of the Goddess? I have. I know that connecting with the Goddess can help you during good times and bad.

For example, my friend, Marisa, does her best to be kind to people. Still, she gets hit by news that her boyfriend cheats on her, her father ends up in the hospital and her manager says she's going to be laid off. All in the same month. Where is Goddess now?

I'm eight years old. My mother forces me to wear dresses for church. I don't like it. My brother, 11 years old, continues to torture me, including the time he held me under water at somebody's pool. I was terrified that I would die. He laughed.

My parents continue to ignore my pleas for protection.

Hidden in the bedroom, I've wrapped yellow yarn around my neck.

I want to die.

Tears running down my face, I move and I hang from the bunk bed post.

At the time, I had only heard of an angry God. The image of a furious man who would hurt me if I broke His rules.

I had no idea that I could turn to the Goddess.

Still, in my time of need at eight years old . . . The yarn snapped. Goddess saved me. And I didn't know She was there. Not yet.

Years later, during one of my meditation sessions, both the Goddess and the God appeared to me. I was a solitary practitioner of Wicca at that time.

My friend, I'm glad to share this book with you.

I've learned in my journey which includes being a Wiccan High Priestess that the Goddess deeply cares for us.

She even reveals secrets. I'm going share 5 *Major Secrets* with you throughout this book.

Let's begin with . . .

SECRET #1: GODDESS WANTS YOU TO ENJOY ABUNDANCE.

I've seen a number of times that Goddess has lined up many blessings for me. Sometimes, I was so caught up in what "I did not have" that I missed all the blessings that I did have.

Then I discovered something. Goddess would give me intuitive ideas, and when I acted on those intuitive ideas, new opportunities would rise up.

For example, I felt called by the Goddess and the God to start my blog GoddessHasYourBack.com. It started from zero and now has visitors from 173 countries. From the blog and working with my editors, I then wrote three books. Sometimes, I find it hard to believe that "little dyslexic me" has written four books with the help of editors.

These books have led to my giving workshops, even one in North Hollywood, California.

Goddess often gives us hints or bits of intuitive ideas. We find that it helps for us to listen and take some steps forward.

CALL UPON THE GODDESS AND ASK FOR ABUNDANCE

My friend, Sandra, braced herself for bad news. It was worse. Not only was her car needing repairs, the cost was so high, it was better to just get another car!

"How am I going to have enough money to get another car?" she asked me.

I've gone through tough times about money, too.

A number of Wiccans I know are lovely people but talk with them long enough, and they talk a lot about *not* having enough money.

What is going on with Wiccans and having troubles about prosperity?

I've even talked with a number of elders in our community. They're talking about fears about getting older. Where will they live and how will they live when they're pushed out of the workforce?

Are there too many of us Wiccans hesitating about calling upon the God and Goddess for help in terms of prosperity?

I even hear about Wiccan friends who say, "You know, I don't have much. But somehow I get what I need. Hey, I found a bus pass today. It was just laying there on the sidewalk."

Here's the point of this section: Two things . . . a) call

upon the Goddess and b) ask for *abundance.*

Is that so hard?

Apparently, it is.

The second element "asking for abundance" can be hard for those of us focused on a spiritual path. We think that it's extravagant or "not spiritual" to ask for more than we need.

And here's the third vital element: *Ask for Goddess's guidance* about how you can serve in better ways so that people want to hire you and provide more money. Not just enough to survive—but an abundance so you can thrive!

I know that this might seem uncomfortable.

I'm uncomfortable about money, too.

But then I remember that we Wiccans are on a spiritual path. Such a path is about serving AND receiving.

One of my friends keeps talking about how "we live in an AND-universe."

So let's use that idea: "We serve AND we receive abundance."

Ask the Goddess to help your magick.

So what kind of magick can be used to increase your prosperity?

You can use Cord Magick, Sigil Magick, Candle Magick and more! [Please see the Section "Secret #4: Goddess will Augment Your Magick."]

Again, I want to emphasize in this section: **Don't just ask to "get by."**

Ask for guidance so you can *manifest financial abundance by being of more service.*

A friend of a friend worked for UPS. And the guy loved building furniture. So he kept the UPS job and, on the weekends, built furniture and sold various pieces.

He had more abundance.

That sounds good to me.

LISTENING TO THE GODDESS AND STEPPING ON YOUR PATH

From my first thoughts of this book, I had the title *Goddess Walks Beside You* in mind. I've learned that we can step forward on a better path as *we listen for guidance* from the Goddess.

The tough part about the Goddess's guidance is that She only gives intuitive ideas for what to do *now*.

It's like we're given steps 1,2,3, but we don't know exactly where we're going in steps 18, 19, 20.

So I've learned to listen to intuitive guidance from the Goddess and do my part. I move forward with Steps 1,2,3.

At Step 3, I can now see what steps 4, 5, 6 are and what I can do next.

This book is designed to support you as you work with your present guidance and take action where you are at this time.

At any moment you might zoom forward.

The Goddess asks us to have faith and do our part in the present moment.

HOW GODDESS FREES YOU FROM WEEDS IN YOUR MIND

"I'm such a f—ing idiot," I yelled.

My friend, Sarah, ran into the kitchen, asking, "What happened?"

"I trashed the recipe. This tastes like crap. I'm no good at anything," I said.

"Who told you that?"

"People," I replied.

"Which people?"

"Everybody," I maintained. "My mother's called my cookies 'hockey pucks.'"

Now, years later, I realize that I had a bunch of automatic-thoughts. Thoughts that tore me down. Our minds are like a bed of fertile soil, and the ideas we have are like seeds.

Before we go any further, I invite you to realize that Goddess wants you to have good seeds/good thoughts. Why? **Goddess wants you to enjoy your life.**

I'm not guessing here. *I know.* During many of my meditations, I felt the real presence of the Goddess—such loving kindness.

It's important to realize that many people—parents, friends, teachers and the media—plant seeds in our minds. **Some seeds are weeds.**

We need to take responsibility for the garden in our mind. We need to learn how to weed out the unhealthy thoughts. We learn to encourage the positive thoughts—the roses. Weeding our own bed of soil (our mind) helps us to be healthy and happy.

So how can we do that? Ask this question: *Is this thought harming or hindering my happiness?* Also ask: *Is this thought/belief making me grow in the direction I want? Or is this thought stunting my growth and making me miserable?*

Take special care to notice the seeds (thoughts) you plant yourself. In many cases, we're still operating with thoughts we planted as children. Every child is different as is every adult who grows up (at least physically).

Have you noticed recently how two people can have opposite reactions to the same event?

For example, Janet hates rain storms because she deems them to be gloomy and the cause of her getting wet hair as she runs to her car.

Janet's best friend Cindy loves the rain because it makes the flowers grow.

Do you see how Janet is planting weeds and Cindy is planting roses?

Here's a secret: In many cases, we can transform the weeds to roses—that is, we can work to change *our perception* of a situation. It does take creativity.

Creativity is the area where Wiccans *thrive*. We Wiccans have tools to use with our creative energies. Cowans (non-magickal folk) only use their brains for creativity (for the most part). On the other hand, Wiccans have spells, chants, meditations and much more to work with.

Here is an example of a chant you can use to transform weed-like thoughts to those that empower you:

Transformation Chant
Poisonous thoughts these weeds of mine,
Keeping me from peace this time.

Plucking my weeds hither and fro,
Weeding my thoughts like a pro.

Now peace and happiness I grow,
Lord and Lady make it so!

I invite you to pay attention to the weeds (negative thoughts) you may find in your mind. Weeds rise up without our efforts.

Instead, tend your garden of your mind and blossom into the empowered version of who you really are.

WHAT IS A SOUL?

"What is a soul?" one of my Facebook friends asked.

This is a powerful question. In fact, I've had a number of conversations with elders in the Wiccan community on this topic.

I'll now share a view that has formed for me out of those conversations and my own intuitive understanding:

In the beginning there was nothing but the Void. Then, with a single thought of "I AM!" the ALL created Itself. But soon, the ALL wanted a new experience, and so the ALL separated Itself into Two. The ALL did this by making a mighty scream. The Dark Half became the Goddess. She in turn gave birth to another entity that, at first was only a wave, but soon, It had thought, and so became Illumination. With illumination, the entity became intelligent, and He was the God, the Light Half to the Goddess.

The God slowly drifted away from the Goddess. Soon after his illumination, the God realized He had been created. He was curious about Who had created Him. He began a search, looking in a circle for the One who had made Him. Soon He realized that His Creator was no where that He had looked. The only place His Creator could be was in the center of the circle. So he went there and met the Goddess.

The Goddess found him brilliant and irresistible. She fell in love with Him. They made love and created all we know and that which we do not yet know.

We start with the ALL and then have the Goddess and the God.

How does this relate to you and I as souls?

A soul is the energy that resides within everything. From people to trees, everything has this sacred energy.

Where does this sacred energy come from?—from the ALL

which yearns to learn about Itself. To understand Itself, the ALL creates small pieces of Itself, which are Its children.

The soul radiates *the life soul energy*. Further, the soul is connected by the different chakras located throughout our bodies.

I'm fascinated by the detail that the life soul energy manifests outward from the chakras as one's aura. Some people can see this aura energy.

A few can see the aura and appreciate it as a guide to heal people. The healer sees via the aura whether the person has health problems. With this knowledge, some healers have clues as to how the person may heal.

It helps to have a view of how things are interconnected.

We, Pagans, understand how all people and beings are *essentially* connected.

* * *

Being a Wiccan witch is hard to explain to those who do not walk this sacred path.

YOU CAN'T KNOW IT UNLESS YOU LIVE IT

Andrew had that look in his eyes. A dash of confusion and a pinch of cynicism. "Tell me. What is Wicca, really?" Andrew asked.

Because I knew Andrew had to leave for an appointment soon, I thought that I'd better boil this down to a few sentences.

Then I thought, *What does Wicca really mean to me?*

Is Wicca just about herbs, brews, crystals and poppets? Or is it something else? How can I sum Wicca up in just a few sentences, or even one sentence?

Could you do it?

Yes, Wicca involves herbs, brews, crystals and more. But that is *not* Wicca. Is it about the Gods, dancing and singing? It does have those, too. But what is Wicca at its core?

The clearest way I can explain Wicca is: It's a *practice.* Wicca is something you *do.* Not something you have. You can have all the trimmings with the crystals, herbs, fancy robes and even a crystal ball. But that does not make you a Wiccan.

Wicca is something you practice *everyday.* Wicca is a *part of you.* It's what you **do**, not what you *have.*

Wicca is honoring the God and Goddess with each breath, and honoring the earth as you walk. It's finding the peace within your mind and heart, and then sharing that with others.

To me **that** is what Wicca is. It is finding the light with the Gods' guidance and reflecting this light for others to find their own way on the path.

I strive to do this everyday. Sometimes I'm right on the mark, doing and breathing Wicca. Sometimes, I'm off. Perhaps, I miss my daily meditation. This is why we look on Wicca as a practice. You continue to develop yourself throughout your life. Sure, at times, you may stumble. But Wicca is about taking each step forward.

You continue walking the Wicca path before you.

Sometimes it's hard; sometimes it's easy.

With the Gods' guidance, it's always true and fulfilling.

THE MANY FACES OF THE GODS

"I don't get it. Why are there so many faces or versions of

the God and Goddess?" my friend, Cara, asked.

"Let me put it into this context. Today is the first of three harvest festivals called Lammas. We collect our bounty at this time, reaping what we had sown in the beginning of the year. This is a wonderful time of family and friends. It's also when we see the Gods grow older and start to wane," I replied.

"Grow older. What's that about? They're Gods. They don't need to grow old," Cara protested.

"True. Still, the Gods are relating to us. They're expressing the Cycles of Life. And Cycles are part of the human experience of birth, maturity and death," I said.

Why do the Gods change and look different at different times of the year and look different to everyone in general?

All over the world, people describe "God" or the God and Goddess in many varied ways. People point to various physical traits and characteristics.

The Gods can look like anything they want to. The Deity that I relate to has the body of a man and the horns of a stag, for example.

At this time, I relate to the Goddess in the form of the Earth Mother. I appreciate how She nurtures us and shares her bounty with us.

Each individual can connect with Goddess in any form. Who's to say that the Goddess isn't black, red, yellow or even blue? She could be a Heron or any other animal or the combination of several creatures.

We notice how Deities differ in appearance from culture to culture. We also have young Gods and Old Gods. These Gods help people understand the life cycles they are in at that particular moment in time.

Young women often relate to the Maiden aspect of the Goddess. Many women in their later years find that they have more in common with the Crone.

The God and Goddess in Their many forms are manifestations of the ALL. The God and Goddess are the Universe—The ALL is a singular entity.

The ALL (the term I will use from now on to represent both masculine and feminine together) wants to connect with Its children—that includes us.

You probably noticed that you simply relate more to certain images, ideas and thoughts. Maybe the Maiden form of the Goddess speaks to you. Perhaps, the Horned God means a lot to you because you feel this glorious connection to nature. The ALL is *every* form of the God and Goddess *at the same time.*

The ALL is the sky and the Earth beneath our feet. It is the forests, the streams, the wind and the howl of the wolf. It is Maiden, Mother and Crone.

So we are never alone, because *we are part of the ALL.*

I believe the ALL split Itself and had children because It wants to know and learn about Itself through the lives of Its children, us. Yes, we have an afterlife and reincarnation. Those are also steps in the ALL learning about Itself.

So I invite you to enjoy learning about the pantheon of Gods and Goddesses.

Discover which form you most relate to now.

Since life is made of Cycles and new chapters, you will have many opportunities to connect with new forms of the God and the Goddess throughout your journey.

WICCA ON A BUDGET

When I first started on the Wiccan path, I read some books and it appeared that I needed a bunch of tools—which

I could not afford! What was I to do? Like many young people at that time, I didn't have a lot of money.

Many books don't tell you something important: You probably already have all the tools you need. You don't need all the fancy trappings and trimmings to practice the Craft. Using something simple is just as effective as employing some store-bought, fancy item. Tools encrusted with gems and other trimmings don't make for a better tool.

In fact, the most powerful tools are ones we make ourselves.

Why? As you make the tool, the tool absorbs your energy and so holds more power.

But do not fear if you're not skilled with arts and crafts. You will do just fine with simple things you gather from within your home.

Which household items can you use for your tools of Wicca?

Avoid items that are made of plastic because plastic does *not* hold spiritual charge. Natural substances can hold a spiritual charge.

Now, here's a list of things you can use:

Altar: Any table will do.

Altar Cloth: A large square scarf (or even sarong) will work. Just remember that the altar cloth helps to keep wax from damaging the altar. So if you do not want wax on your cloth, find some other material.

Athame: You can use a butter knife. Generally an athame is a black-handled, double edged knife. But a butter knife will work just fine. An athame doesn't need to be sharp. It cuts energy not material things.

Bell: Any bell will work. You can even use a utensil to strike a wine glass. The bell on a cat collar will also work.

Boline: The traditional boline is a white handled knife

often with a curved blade, but a steak knife will work well. This knife, unlike the athame, is used for cutting physical things like herbs. You'll also use the boline to carve runes and names on candles.

Candles: Any kind of candles will do. Further, any inexpensive tea lights would work.

Cauldron: Any fireproof container will do. A pot works well.

Censer: A simple bowl of sand will work just fine.

Goblet or chalice: Any glass will do. A wine glass will work well. Originally, the traditional goblet was made out of wood.

Incense: You could use fresh herbs from your garden if you don't have regular incense.

Offering Dishes: The bowls from your kitchen cabinet will work just fine.

Pentacle: A simple plate painted with a pentagram works. Pentacles were often made out of carved wax, which could be thrown in a fire and melted into nothing. That's one way that witches employed to stay hidden from the wrath of persecutors.

Salt: It's nice to have sea salt, but table salt will do.

Wand: A branch from a tree in your garden will work. Make sure it does not touch the ground as this would cause the loss of the power the tree gave it.

Water: You don't need to have spring water. Tap water works fine.

As you can see, most if not all of the tools you need reside in your home already. If you can make your own tools, that's even better. However, most of us are not metalsmiths, nor do we have a forge handy. That's okay, since I shared handy substitute-items above.

Wicca can be done on a budget. All you need is your

imagination.

* * *

One thing I have noticed in the Pagan community in general is that everyone wants to be unique and find their own style. We all want to be our own person. We choose specific clothes, jewelry, makeup and music. Some people are drawn to a specific form of art and the related rituals . . .

WICCANS AND TATTOOS—
A SPIRITUAL JOURNEY

I leaned forward, tensing a bit as the needle found its mark. The ink started creating the wings of a butterfly, with my cat Magick's cute eyes included in those wings.

A number of Wiccans like to decorate their temple—that is, their body. Some Wiccans create whole rituals around getting tattooed.

My getting a back tattoo was an expression of my spiritual journey. My tattoo's imagery includes the journey of a caterpillar to butterfly. My multiple sessions in the chair became *my* rite, to myself and to the Gods. As the needle continued to pierce my skin, I silently chanted.

Why get a tattoo? Many people use tattoos as a way to express who they are. The tattoos tell their story. For example, I have a dedication to my spirit guide as one tattoo.

Getting a tattoo does hurt. For me, it's a trial to endure, or a sacrifice, as part of my personal rite of passage.

If you consider having a tattoo done, realize you can include words, images, sigils and more. It's sacred art. Let your spiritual imagination flow. Further, think long and hard about the placement of your tattoo. Who will you let see your sacred art? Will you be careful and make sure that a shirt can cover your tattoo so you have more possibilities for employment? (Yes, some employers still have an aversion to tattoos.)

Is your tattoo only to be visible to yourself and your coven?

Some people choose to place a sigil on their arm (for example) so they can see it often and thus recharge it. Others choose to place a tattoo somewhere that they do not see often.

A tattoo involves many questions and requires lots of thinking and feeling. Be sure to connect with your own intuition. For some people a tattoo is *not* part of their path.

Take care before or *if* you decide to get spiritually inked.

CHANGING AND GROWING ON MY PATH

The video camera "record light" glowed red, and I asked the notable witch a powerful question: *What has changed in your belief system from when you started?*

This question resonated in my thoughts. When I first started my practice of Wicca, I read that the Gods were everywhere. I just went along with that but I didn't function on the level of really *knowing* this.

I didn't intend to fall into a pattern of looking upon the authors as all knowing priests, telling me what to think and how to worship. (Even if the authors did not mean to "preach," I took their words in that way.) This is *not* the spirit of the Craft. If you want to be *told what to do and how to do it* for your spiritual path, go to certain churches, synagogues or other places of worship.

Wicca is something different. Because I lacked experience, my perception of the Craft was off. As I mentioned, the authors seemed liked preachers to me. The Craft is **not** a faith of listening to someone standing at a pulpit and following what they say.

But when I first started out I treated my practice of Wicca like that. I lacked the understanding and more importantly, *knowing* the Gods. Once I *met* the Gods, my understanding became a *knowing* in my heart what the Craft is really about.

Instead of looking outward toward Deity, which is what many of the mainstream religions do, I looked *within*. I found a new world to explore. Looking within, I could no longer deny that my thoughts of inferiority and self-loathing were *not* the truth of the Gods. Such thoughts of self-loathing were the fruit of abuse and my frightened ego.

The experience of meeting the Gods during my meditation gave me a whole new sight. This sight was of the love and compassion of the Gods. I saw myself as They see me: a creation of beauty.

The Gods communicated to me *specifically* that They crafted all Their children with love, respect and reverence. So much so that They put themselves into each one of us.

Since that time, I have grown with the knowing that Deity is within *and* throughout the world around us.

Some might suggest that this insight is a "no-brainer," but the truth is: I really needed to learn this firsthand through interacting with the Gods.

Just reading or listening to others tell me about this insight was *not* enough. I needed to *experience* the real *teaching moment* for me.

Now I look within to *hear* the Gods and look outside me to see the signs from the Gods. I have a personalized relationship with the Goddess and God. They are my friends and confidants. They lead me and guide me through my everyday life, including crucial times of hardship.

My journey has also included starting as a solitary witch and then joining a coven.

Like many people I started by reading books. At the time, I couldn't find a mentor and I wanted to have the right mentor. So I asked the Gods for Their help. They responded, "… when you're ready."

So I stayed on the solitary path for many years—reading many books and practicing the Craft as well as I could.

Finally, my first mentor arrived in my life. The Gods were right. I had finally had enough knowledge so that I was able to more fully appreciate my first mentor's guidance.

Through my first mentor, I had my first experiences as a member of a coven. It was nice to turn to someone who had the experience I lacked. My mentor would steer me on the safest and fastest path that was right for me. All along the way I still talked to the Gods and worked with Them to tailor the lessons of my journey.

To this day, I still ask my mentors for their guidance.

CHAPTER TWO:
SECRET #2: GODDESS CAN BE REACHED FOR HER GUIDANCE

In Chapter 1, we learned of *Secret #1: Goddess wants you to enjoy abundance.*

It makes sense that Goddess would give you *some help* to create more abundance in your life.

This leads us to **Secret #2: Goddess can be reached for Her Guidance.**

You could put this book down, sit in a quiet place and just focus on your breathing.

Sometimes, I do meditating by doing something as simple as that.

In such a simple meditation, it's possible for you to receive an intuitive idea from Goddess that might set you into a new chapter of abundance.

Goddess's guidance can also arrive through a book like this or something you happen to overhear while sitting in a public place and eating your lunch.

The point is to step into each new day with sacred faith

and a certain openness to hearing guidance from the Goddess.

Sometimes, Goddess invites you to receive guidance through your Spirit Guides.

HOW TO MEET YOUR SPIRIT GUIDES

"How can I meet my Spirit Guides?" Jessie asked.

"Through meditation," I replied. "While meditating, I had this experience:

I went to the standing stones and asked to meet my Spirit Guide. Suddenly, I was aware of a loving presence. A beautiful woman came forward. She approached me, and I could see her pleasant features form. Lovely brown hair and eyes came into focus. She reached out and took my hand."

You can receive guidance from your Spirit Guide or even a Totem Animal.

Shaman Elder Maggie Wahls wrote: "A totem animal is often a protector, a mate to travel the Inner Worlds with who knows its way around and can get you in, to your destination and out again safely."

I always start in a safe place on the astral plane. This could be a cottage or a circle of standing stones. Pick a place that has power to protect you. You can meet your Spirit Guide there.

The Witches' Cottage is where I start in my daily meditation. From the Witches' Cottage you can begin your journey on the astral plane.

At first, I was going to list the Witches' Cottage meditation here. Then, in discussion with my own mentor, certain concerns arose. She said, "The first time should be with a knowledgeable practitioner who can get the person out of the trance if there's a problem."

Following my mentor's advice, I am now going to discuss *what happens* during such a meditation.

With the help of a knowledgeable practitioner, you start in a cottage and then go to a circle of stones (called standing stones). Then you meet the Goddess (or your Spirit Guide) there. Then you return to the cottage and ultimately open your eyes, having returned from your journey on the astral plane.

The Witches' Cottage serves as a safe place when you start traveling on the astral plane.

My process is to begin at my Witches' Cottage and then go to the standing stones.

Now I can address a couple of details: a) finding a knowledgeable practitioner to guide you and b) how to stay safe on the astral plane.

a) Finding a knowledgeable practitioner

In the *Bonus Chapter: How to Find a Mentor ... and More,* I go into detail about finding the right person for you. Here I want to mention that, with a knowledgeable practitioner to guide you, you can grow much faster. Further, the mentor can show you how to avoid pitfalls and big mistakes.

b) How to stay safe on the astral plane.

The knowledgeable practitioner can pull you back to the mundane world. Some time later, after you have become quite skilled, you can use a number of techniques to defend yourself on the astral plane. For example, when you get a new athame, bless and consecrate it and complete a dedication ritual, you are, in essence, making a copy of this athame on the astral plane. Now, that you have this copy, you can use it for defense when you are on the astral plane.

WHAT PAGANS KNOW

When I arrived at Pinecrest campground, I looked forward to hiking through the pine trees until . . . my heart broke, seeing all of the dying trees.

Sure, we Californians complain about cutting back on our water consumption amid cries of "Drought!"

But I did not feel it in my gut until I saw all the brown, dying trees.

The trees all over California are dying.

What does this have to do with Wicca?

We can notice that the human race, for the most part, has neglected our Sacred Mother Earth. Many have ignored the God and the Goddess or downright forgotten about Them.

Mother Earth is sick, and we need to come to Her aid. What can we do?

We can protect her. Walking, bicycling, carpooling when possible. My sweetheart often takes the train and avoids commuting by car. Be sure to recycle and consider eating locally grown food.

We can also gather with others and organize a clean-up Mother Earth day or afternoon. Then you would pick up trash at beaches, forests, or even your own neighborhood.

I believe we need to fight global warming on a personal level, and in groups. Small actions do make a difference.

In a another section, I talk about how a friend and I cleaned up a big mess left by previous campers. It really bothered me that those individuals thought they could leave their trash and waste anywhere they pleased. They took no responsibility for their actions.

Pagans know better. My friend and I went into immediate action and cleaned up the campsite. The rangers were quite happy to provide us with bags to assist our "be kind to

Mother Earth" actions.

Now I invite you to get involved on some level.

Let us, Pagans, lead by example.

Let's show others on this beautiful Mother Earth how to be good stewards with the gifts we have been given.

HOW A WICCAN RECOVERS HER BALANCE

As Wiccans, we make continuous efforts to stay in balance with nature. Right now much of the western U.S. is suffering through a heat wave.

Staying cool is important—not just as a convenience but staying cool can save your life! So we're turning up the AC (air conditioning) now.

As Wiccans, we endure other situations which throw us off balance and which require another form of "AC." Whether you're confronted with an argument with a family member or some driver cutting you off in traffic, you can see your temper getting frayed.

In fact, I'm concerned about keeping cool and not getting irritable with others (even if they deserve it).

So how do you turn on your own AC during these heated times?

Breath control is a great way to calm down and control your words and actions.

Let's say your stressed out and you're losing your cool. What can you do?

Breathe. Let's practice now. Take in a deep breath through your nose. In your mind count three (a sacred number) slowly.

Hold your breath for two counts. And then breathe out for three counts.

Repeat this slowly through five repetitions.

How do you feel now? Many of us find ourselves calming down. That's really useful!

Remember breath control as your personal AC in a heated situation.

What happens when we don't use breath control and we do something that we regret at a later date? Next, I'll share how to deal with regret.

HOW A WICCAN GETS FREE OF REGRET

I toss and turn in the bed. The same thoughts, the same regrets run again in my mind.

Why did I do that?! How stupid!

Do regrets keep you awake and haunt your day-time thoughts?

Sometimes, I get stuck with thoughts of regret and pain.

How can you release these painful thoughts?

You could try to take a rational approach. Maybe saying to yourself, "Oh. It's not so bad." However, many of us discover that merely ignoring such thoughts ultimately keeps them around!

Instead, I invite you to take a look. (You might need support. A trusted friend or even a counselor.)

You can resolve to really look at the regret. Feel some of the pain. And then resolve to *start a process of letting go.*

Ask yourself these questions:

- What did I learn from this past experience?
- If I need to, can I make amends? If so, how?
- If I can't make amends for some reason, what is the next best thing I might do?

After you have answered these questions with a truthful heart, chant these words:

Release the Regret Chant
Regret of mine, running though my mind.
This moment I leave the past behind
Now Leave my mind
No more to bind
I release you
I release me
By sky, stars, sun and moon
This regret leaves real soon
By candlelight, I now clear the space
The open spot Goddess fills with grace

Envision the regretful thought. Give it a color. Imagine the thought floating away, leaving you with *space*. Fill this space with the Gods' light. Feel the peace now present.

If this process does not fully work for you the first time, stay with it.

Repeat the process.

And do not hesitate to ask the God and the Goddess for help.

They want you to be free and fully present in each new moment.

OPEN THE DOOR FOR LOVE

"You can have that piece of sushi," Paul said.

"No, that one is yours," Rachel said.

"Go ahead."

"Why?" she asked.

"Come on. It's Valentine's Day."

"Well. Okay!" Rachel said, smiling and popping the food in her mouth.

In the USA, we celebrate Valentine's Day, a holiday when we focus on being loving to a spouse or sweetheart.

But so many of us forget the most important person in our lives during this holiday. Who is the most important person to you? It's *you.*

Do you feel too busy to pause and even acknowledge your feelings? Do you lack time to show some loving care for yourself?

I spend *so much time* worrying about what other people think and feel. Are my friends okay? Is my mother irritated with me again? Is my father having trouble understanding people because he has a mild form of Alzheimer's?

I've learned something important: Neglecting ourselves can really get us into trouble.

It's even more extreme for those of us who have self-esteem issues. Some of us spiral down and need assistance from mental health professionals.

For example, I have struggled with self-hate and loathing my whole life so far because I deal with the symptoms of my depression.

There are times when I feel so depressed that I find it nearly impossible to demonstrate love and affection for my loved ones. At those times, I have retreated to my bed.

I've learned that I must practice self-care or I have no energy to be loving and kind to important people in my life.

Loving others must arise from being kind and loving to yourself.

I have learned that *you need to love yourself before you can truly love another person.*

How can we begin or reignite our journey of being loving,

including loving ourselves? In my book, *Goddess Has Your Back*, I share the Self-Love meditation. This meditation really set me on a correct course.

In this section, I'll now share a process to help you enhance your self-love.

Self-Love and Self-Esteem Ritual

What you will need:

- Pen
- 3 sheets of paper
- Fireproof container
- Lighter

Take the first two sheets and place them on a table before you.

Label one sheet: "How I like myself." Write things you that like about yourself. If you're feeling a bit low, just include small things like: "I like how I finish reading an article. I like that I call my sister just to say hello." Write *at least five things* down or even ten things.

Label the second sheet of paper: "Things I want to change —Things I'm not happy with." Write some things that you want to change or that you're not happy about. Write a minimum of two things and *no more* than five.

Many of us will notice that our "not happy" list might feel "more important" or more intense. That's understandable.

Now, we will use the third sheet. Look at both previous lists. There may be some overlap. For example, your second sheet may include something like: "I screw up everything." But at the same time, your first sheet says, "I take good care of my sweetheart." Is one true and the other false?

Is the "screw up everything" true because you find that you feel bad much of the time? Perhaps, it's possible that your perception is off. I've learned from my own mentors that my depression symptoms can warp my perception and have me do something called "catastrophizing." That means I might take one thought and let it overrun everything. For example, one time I was late in picking up my sweetheart. He remained in the rain and cold for 15 minutes. At the train stop, there was no shelter. I thought, "I'm thoughtless. I'm no good. I'm incompetent."

Other vicious words swirled through my mind. However, the truth was that I'm on time or even early 199 times out of 200. That is the truth. But my perception was off.

So you'll now use the third sheet to dispel perceptions that are off. Increase your positive feelings and demonstrate some self-love. Write down healthy perceptions. In essence, you combine the ideas in a fundamentally positive way.

For example, it could look like this: "I'm good to my sweetheart" plus "I screw up everything" becomes *"I'm good to my sweetheart and <u>sometimes</u> I make a mistake. I can learn to do better."*

Go through the lists and complete at least three "positive and combined healthy perceptions."

The next step:

Gather your fireproof container, your lighter and the "I'm not happy about" list. You will soon safely burn the "I'm not happy about" list.

Hold the "not happy" list over the fireproof container. Light the paper and let it drop into the container. Say,

My list of unwanted traits I hold,
harming my love for myself I'm told.
Now I release these thoughts to the light
burning now forever from my life.
Fire transform this list I hold tonight,

I now have self-love to its fullest height.

The next step:
The two positive lists "How I like myself" and "Healthy Perceptions" are gifts you have given yourself.

Look at the healthy perceptions and *think of one small thing* you might do that can help you improve your life.

Self-love is NOT self-obsession nor conceit. Self-love is recognizing that the God and Goddess have made you with positive traits for your joy and blessings to those people near you.

God and Goddess stand ready to support you. Simply ask for Their Support.

FACING LOVE, LIFE, AND DEATH

On August 11, 2014, Robin Williams committed suicide. This really hit home for me. Being a person who has lived on both sides of the suicide-situation, I feel that it's time I talk about it.

I have attempted multiple times to commit suicide in my life. I've often felt the unspeakable pain that drives one to such thoughts and actions.

The truth is: A lot of people have no way of comprehending the emotions of the person considering suicide. As a friend said to me, "It's similar to grief. You do NOT know it, until you're IN grief. Until someone close to you has died."

On the other side of the situation, I have also endured when a very dear friend committed suicide. My heartbreak seared deeper than any hot poker could. Searing my flesh would have been a kindness. This pain of grief hits you deep in the soul.

Recently, I was appalled at how some pundit on a cable channel called Robin Williams "a coward" for taking his own life. Did this pundit personally know Robin? Does this pundit struggle with depression personally?

And I have other questions.

Is it possible that depression can become an unbearable pain? (I have felt such pain and fortunately the Gods broke the cord that could have ended my life.)

Is it possible that it is the right of each individual to choose how to live and how and when to die?

And then let's add the spiritual questions.

Does the person on the verge of suicide feel (or care) that one will have to come back (be reincarnated) and learn the same thing he or she was struggling with and go through it all over again?

If suicidal thoughts arise for you, *do you want to go through it again* (in a reincarnated form)? Or hunker down and go through it once? (I know that to press on through suicidal thoughts can require professional and medical help.)

Still, I feel compassion for someone who has succumbed to suicide's call.

I am not angry at my deceased friend. I only feel sorrow for him and that I could not help. I try not to blame myself for possibly missing a sign or two that he was in distress.

If you are having thoughts of suicide, please call the hotline below.

1-800-273-TALK (8255)

Or go to the web sites
USA: http://www.suicide.org/suicide-hotlines.html

International: http://www.suicide.org/international-suicide-hotlines.html

LOOKING WITHIN AND FINDING CONTROL IN YOUR LIFE

I'm gasping for breath in the ER, yet again, hit by my asthma, hearing a man on meth scream at the top of his lungs in Spanish. I wonder when the doctor will come and help me. I'm thinking, "Please don't put me on prednisone again."

I have been on prednisone three times in the past month and a half. Each time I've gained significant weight because of the medication.

I seem to be losing my battle of the bulge. *I just want to be healthy.*

Losing weight would help me in so many ways. Not only would my body be happy but my mind would be free from the burden of worrying about diabetes. I'd just be happy to move easily.

So why is it not in my cards?

The meth-man behind the curtain wrenches at his restraints and screams profanities in Spanish. That's when it hits me . . .

I'm the screaming man. I'm in a situation I cannot control, tethered to my asthma, angry as hell.

The doctor comes in and orders two nebulizer treatments and puts me back on prednisone. Again!

I can't stop my asthma, it is something I don't control. **So what can I control?**

What goes in my body

Yes, I need strong medications. But I can control my intake of food and drink. I'll eat what the God and Goddess provides such as natural vegetables and fruits instead of artificial foods. (Donuts are my bane.)

Moving my body

Yes, it is more difficult to exercise; it's hard to breathe. But I can move some each day. It doesn't have to be overtaxing so I have an asthma attack. *Any movement is good.* Walking in the beauty of the world that the Gods have created is good for us, and the Gods especially like it when we appreciate their handiwork.

Getting rest

Getting rest to heal is just as important as movement. Getting adequate rest lessens my asthma problems. I am going to increase time for meditation, which will soothe my brain, body and soul.

Feeling Some Comfort

Understanding I have power in these three areas is comforting. I can't control the side effects of the drugs I take. *But there are things I can do.*

Concentrating on what I can do in these three areas raises my morale. I can practice letting go of worries about what I cannot control.

This brings moments of happiness to my daily life.

I invite you to look at the two areas: What can you control? And what is completely out of your control?

When you get clear about these distinctions and you bring your efforts to the Gods, you'll find some comfort.

You deserve it.

HOW A WICCAN CAN GET HEALTHIER

Out of breath after walking up some stairs, I thought: "I got to do better than this." I had succumbed to gaining serious extra weight.

Then, I noted an app on my new Smartphone—a pedometer. A number of doctors/researchers emphasize that walking 10,000 steps a day is valuable.

So I started walking at least 10,000 steps a day. At first, I was okay. And I even limited my intake of fat-adding foods.

The result? Weight loss.

But now I'm enduring more pain in my legs. And it feels tougher and tougher to get out there and keep up my walking regimen.

When you're enduring pain, it can feel like you're all alone.

But wait, I'm Wiccan. I can call upon the Gods for help.

A Simple Rite so You Can Ask the Gods for help.
What you will need: 1 red candle.
Cast Circle in the usual way.
Cleanse & consecrate the candle (cense & asperge candle).
Light the candle and say:

Lord and Lady give me strength to step into the light that is for me. The light of health and strength. Help me keep my stride on this path of light to the best that I can be. And if I falter, lend me Your hands so that I may rise again and continue on my path. Give me the strength to endure and succeed over the challenges of temptation, as I choose to let go of bad habits and improve my health.

So mote it be!

Then do your Cakes and Wine ceremony.

Close Circle in the usual way.

May this ritual be useful for all of us who seek to improve our health.

USING RITUAL TO MARK OUR MOMENTS

Some time ago, I had just finished my first book.

"We should celebrate!" my sweetie said, honoring that I had endured a huge rite of passage to become a published author.

Many Wiccans are familiar with a wiccaning, which is a ritual of showing a baby to the Gods. Another rite of passage is croning, the transition a woman makes into her elder-years.

However, how many of us consider the other major transitions or accomplishments of our lives?

Many of us go through life and skip devising a ritual to honor a major transition of life. We either feel too tired or lack the understanding of how important our recent accomplishment is to our journey.

So how do we recognize and mark an accomplishment?

Composing and doing a ritual is helpful.

It may be as complicated as the labyrinth that held the Minotaur or as *simple* as lighting a candle.

The elements of a good ritual are:

Use the five senses

The most important thing is to make the ritual meaningful to you. A good ritual includes stimulating the five senses.

Some methods to use for your ritual:

Smell: Use your favorite smell like baked cookies, incense, clean sheets, or flowers.

Sight: Use your favorite color or images. Maybe you like kittens, puppies or horses.

Sound: Use a favored piece of music. Perhaps you like pan flute music or classical music.

Touch: Use special robes, including feathers. Sit on a special pillow.

Taste: Enjoy your favorite food and drink for your Cakes and Wine Ceremony (near the end of your ritual).

It's vital to make your ritual personal. Don't just use a generic rite noted in a book. Use your imagination! Remember a ritual is like a sandwich. We'll use the metaphor and note these details: the top slice, the meat and the bottom slice of bread.

1) The top slice: Make sure there is a *definite beginning.*

Mark the beginning with a good memorable action—the ring of a bell or chime. Announce why you're holding the ritual. It's important for everyone to be clear on why they're doing ritual, even if you're the only one participating.

2) Provide the meat, that is, a *middle.*

Here is where you place the acknowledgement of your accomplishment into your ritual. This can be as simple as reading a poem or chanting. You could beat a drum or dance or do both.

3) The bottom slice. Have a *definite end.*

You can use the bell or chime to signal the end of your ritual. Do the Cakes and Wine Ceremony to help you ground yourself.

If you are doing your ritual with friends, you might say, "Please share any words of congratulations if you feel moved to do so at this time."

* * *

We go through different chapters in our life. It's not just the "big moments" like graduation or getting married. You actually rise up different levels in your life.

Be sure to recognize and celebrate your achievements with rituals.

HOW YOU CAN HEAL: ALTERNATIVE MEDICINE VS. MODERN MEDICINE

"Get yourself to a doctor," my dentist said. He just saw bruises in my mouth, and he knew it was the sign for something serious.

Soon I saw my doctor who had me go through some tests. An hour later, I was on the phone with the doctor who said that the tests indicated that *I should go immediately to the emergency room!*

Many Wiccans like to use alternative medicine instead of modern medicine. But how do we use alternative medicine wisely? I've personally used catnip tea for reducing a fever.

I've also used salty water for gargling when having a sore throat.

I'm suggesting that this is an "and" situation. You can use both alternative medicine *and* modern medicine. Sure, we Wiccans sometimes use ancient herbal lore from our ancestors. And still, there's a definite time for modern medicine.

Back to my time in the emergency room. Further tests revealed that I had Idiopathic Thrombocytopenic Purpura or ITP. This is an affliction in which my spleen destroyed my platelets so that my blood did not clot. I was informed that if I bumped into something, I could bleed out!

During my hospitalization, I had to recline on a special air mattress because a regular mattress gave me bruises. It got so bad that I had bruises in the shape of the physicians' hands from when they examined me.

ITP was an affliction that could not be solved by simple herbs.

After one month in the hospital, I endured a splenectomy (the removal of my spleen). *This saved my life.*

Again, I'm suggesting that we look upon alternative medicine *and* modern medicine as part of our toolkit. If I have the sniffles, I might start with teas. However, I'm so glad that I followed the advice of my dentist.

I feel that we, modern Wiccans, have the advantage of both herbal remedies for small afflictions and modern medicine when you need it.

HOW YOU CAN LET GO
OF FEARING DEATH

Do you fear death? Do you wonder what lies on the other side?

Several years ago, in the hospital, I was at death's door. I had Idiopathic Thrombocytopenic Purpura (ITP). ITP is a bleeding disorder which can cause a person to bleed out simply by bumping into furniture. I could hemorrhage in my brain at any time and die instantly. When my dentist saw bruising inside my mouth, he told me to *immediately go to the Emergency Room*.

ITP creates the death's door situation by having the immune system destroying platelets, which are necessary for normal blood clotting. After the first night I stayed at the hospital, the next morning I had bruises all down my body from lying on the bed. I had to remain sitting even while I slept. Because my brain could have hemorrhaged and killed me, I got to know death's call intimately. Death was there every day, sitting by my side waiting with me.

I had to accept that death could take me at anytime.

At first I was afraid. But then I realized that death is just a transition, not an ending.

Death is a transition to the Summerlands, a wonderful place of comfort and peace. Your family and friends who went before are there. Who could fear that?

When I first heard of the Summerlands, a complete knowing came to me. And, I also realized that that this place of comfort and peace is where we came from. So you don't need to fear returning to where you came from. When we die, we go home.

And, once you return home, you can choose to be born

again. Wiccans know this as reincarnation.

So as you connect with the idea and reality of the Summerlands, you can let go of fears about dying. Death is simply a transition to a place of rest, loved ones and renewal to prepare you for the next life, if you so choose.

Understanding that now, I do not fear death.

INVITE THE GODS TO COMFORT YOU

"I'm feeling overwhelmed a lot of the time. Sometimes, I'm afraid but I'm not clear about what's really bothering me," Nadine, a close friend, said.

Since that conversation, I've reflected on this human dilemma. We have all had trouble in which we see bad circumstances pile up against us.

However, sometimes we know that some trouble is present, but we can't see the details clearly.

One way to see our obstacles clearly is to do a Candle-Lighting Ritual.

Light the candle and concentrate on the candle's flame. Recite this chant:

The Gods' Presence Chant
Though the darkness presses in,
I know the Gods' presence within.
Open the Door for my Insights' flight,
May this be solved in a fortnight.

When you make time to do a ritual, you open the door to feel comforted by the Gods.

CHAPTER THREE:
SECRET #3: YOU CAN ENJOY MORE MOMENTS OF YOUR LIFE WHEN YOU ALIGN WITH GODDESS

In Chapter Two, we learned about the essence of our soul. We are part of the ALL as manifested by the God and the Goddess.

The Divine created you with a divine purpose and design. Here is **Secret #3: You can enjoy more moments of your life when you align with Goddess.**

Getting aligned with the Goddess can happen at any time. You could simply shift your thoughts in a Goddess-y direction.

Goddess celebrates life.

If you're in a low mood, you might decide to ask Goddess for help:

Goddess, give clarity to my thoughts.
That they bring joy and peace to

myself and others.
Show me Your Light in every moment.

Now, we'll explore other ways to align yourself with the Goddess.

HELPING THE GODDESS

My friend, John, drives the lead car and I follow in mine. We're going on a camping trip. This one will be different, we're going "disperse camping," that is, we're not using a public campground. I'm tired, but there's hope! John flicks his blinker on and we turn off the road. *Finally*, no more driving. We step out of our cars and look around. The site turns my stomach.

There is trash *everywhere*, whole bags of it strewn across the forest, even a latrine. Yuck! Some campers just left all their trash; it had to have been quite a large group by how much trash was still there.

What would you do?

We had the option to find another spot. But as a Wiccan, I have a duty to Mother Earth.

Clearing some of the garbage we managed to set up camp. Then we drove to the ranger station down the road and told the rangers of the deplorable conditions of the site.

Then we did something they weren't expecting. We asked for garbage bags so we could clean up the site. Their shocked but pleased faces told the story. They were quite happy to give us as many bags as we wanted.

Back at the camp site, we picked up the garbage along the river and then moved on to the camp area.

Six large and very full trash bags later, the site looked much better. I could feel the Goddess smiling.

On the other hand, it truly saddens me that some people could do this to their Mother.

As witches, Wiccans and pagans, we care for our Mother. With this attitude much of our community cherishes an opportunity to clean Mother Earth.

You don't have to look far and wide for such an opportunity. Just walk your own neighborhood. Or go to a local park. You'll find plenty to clean and improve.

I personally feel a duty to keep my Mother clean and healthy.

How about you?

This is another way to show the Gods respect and love.

* * *

Taking care of the Goddess is one of the more important things Wiccans do. We also need to help *ourselves* recover sometimes.

I imagine that you've faced situations in which someone was unkind or even cruel toward you.

It's important to continually purify and restore you energy so you can handle tough situations.

If you feel angry, be sure to take action to recover your balance . . .

HOW A WICCAN ENJOYS NATURE – IN AND OUT OF THE CITY

"Do you really have to take a week away now? You know I can't get the time away from work," Paul said to his beloved girlfriend, Rachel.

"I know. But I've had this time at Yosemite booked for months now. And you know that nature is where I connect with the Gods."

Do you have a family member or a close friend who doesn't understand that you need to be out in nature to feel whole?

Many people don't understand that we Wiccans go out into the natural world where it is easier for us to connect to Deity. Granted, you can connect anywhere but nature inspires us. As Wiccans we crave it; no, we need it.

Feeling our feet on the bare earth gives us an unencumbered connection to the Gods. The asphalt of city streets is just another barrier.

In the city, you get all your minerals in one breath.

Nature is kinder to our breathing—especially to those of us with asthma. (Can I get a Blessed Be?!)

With extended practice, Wiccans can connect to nature even if standing on asphalt. But we find standing on the bare earth more satisfying than on the concrete jungle most of us live in. It's true that many urban Wiccans find it hard to make time for excursions out into natural settings. Obstacles can include work, commitments to family and friends and simply lacking energy.

Still, communing in nature is important to Wiccans like the next breath to an asthmatic having an attack.

What Wiccans Do In Nature

- Walk and talk to the trees
- Meditate in a field of wildflowers
- Star gaze
- Talk to the Goddess when the moon rises
- Collect herbs (if it is legal where one is walking)

- Talk to the animals
- Ask the Gods to reveal signs to help one improve one's life
- Just breathe
- Commune with the God and Goddess through meditation or observing signs.

If you can't make it to the woods, you can visit a park. You can still commune with the local flora and fauna. Most parks have trees and maybe a few squirrels.

Consider adding a bird feeder if you have a backyard. Plant flowers that attract birds and butterflies. Dedicate the corners of your garden to the four elements. Depending on the size of your backyard, you might set up a gazebo with meditation pillows and a small stone altar.

If you don't have a garden, you can set up a windowsill planter box. Growing herbs and working the soil of your tiny garden still help you connect with nature. You can use the herbs in your Craft work.

Consider adding a daily walk outside to your life. Spending so much time in front of the computer and living a sedentary life, I started to have trouble. It got so bad that I could barely walk a block before pain in my feet and legs would shut down my daily exercise.

Fortunately, in recent months, I take a daily walk. I do enjoy seeing the neighborhood trees and the sky. I'm getting healthier.

"AN IT HARM NONE" WHY?

"I don't understand. *The Wiccan Rede* of 'An it harm none' seems almost impossible," Nadia said.

"Impossible?" I asked.

"Look, I eat fish and chicken. That harms something," Nadia said.

"Okay. I understand what you're talking about. How about this? When you're talking to a family member, and he says something in an irritated way, do you try to escalate it? Do you try to say something worse—something mean?"

"You know I don't. I try to be kind to people," Nadia said.

"Now, you're onto something. 'An it harm none' is in the same spirit as 'be kind; be compassionate.'" I replied.

In Wicca, we're *not* scrambling for "commandments." Wicca is a path that asks us to think, not just blindly obey someone else's orders. This is what attracts many people to Wicca in the first place.

So let's continue with the Wicca approach of thinking (not blind obedience):

Let's look at a hypothetical situation. Emily's home is invaded by an attacker. If "An it harm none" was a commandment, do you think Emily would not fight back?

What if the attacker approaches Emily's nine-year-old son, Joseph?

Many of us would say, go for it Emily and protect your son! And it would work, in a way, with "An it harm none." How? If Emily does nothing, perhaps, Joseph dies. That is a *greater* harm.

Many of us would say, fighting back and causing harm to the attacker is correct—to save a life.

Self-defense appears right in line with *The Wiccan Rede*.

We need to think things through. We know that the world is *not* simply black and white. We don't just turn the other cheek. We live in a shades-of-gray universe.

As we walk our sacred path, we make many decisions with each step we take. Each person has his or her own gait and stride. Each of us has our own moral compass, and we must make our own decisions as to where we place our feet.

I invite you to consider some important issues. Where is the larger amount of harm? Is this a situation in which some form of self-defense is appropriate?

Think of "An it harm none" as an invitation for you to live with as much kindness and compassion as possible.

FACE DANGER AND HARM NONE

The insect stung me and soon my whole arm was swollen. That was several years ago.

Today, I stood facing wasps on my balcony, a can of insecticide in my hand.

For three years, I have dreaded this day. And for three years, I've practiced *The Wiccan Rede* "an it harm none."

But today, the nest is so big and the wasps are so active.

Worse yet, **they're now getting into the house!** Somehow, they are defying our screens and working their way into the house. I must take action.

If I get stung, I feel that my family will need to rush me to a hospital.

The Wiccan Rede advises me to "harm none" but these insects are invaders and they can severely harm me and my family members.

What can I do?

How do we, Wiccans, keep to *The Wiccan Rede* and still live our lives?

Let's look at the word "rede." Its origin is Middle English, and the definition is: "to give counsel to, or to advise." Notice it isn't defined as a *rule*, meaning something that must be followed.

And here is an important point: If I do nothing then *harm will come to me and a family member*. That is NOT "harm none."

So now, it's impossible to follow the "harm none" phrase like a rule.

To simply live, your body is defending you from germs and viruses. That means, your body is killing germs and viruses each day. To survive, you need to eat. Even if you are a vegan, you still kill plants in order to live.

Let's go back to the definition of *rede* and the section that says, "to advise." The idea of "advice" means that a person can take the advice and current circumstances all into account.

So how do I deal with the wasps?

I knock down their nests. I faced the risk of being near them as I was de-homing them. *But they kept coming back.* So I asked in the form of a prayer, "Wasps, please leave."

The wasps did *not* comply with my plea. Over and over they came back and built new nests.

We are still in negotiations at this time.

But you can see: Staying true to my Wiccan path does *not* mean I never act to protect myself. But I strive to follow the Rede as much as I can.

What would you do?

May you find your answers on your path.

SEE THE TRUTH

"Now, do you believe?!" my sweetie said to me, as the plane lifted from the ground.

"Yeah, I do," I replied.

For months, he said that we would take a plane, cross the

country and then take a ship and finally walk on the ocean floor.

Because of dealing with depression symptoms, it was hard for me to really believe that our trip would actually take place. In a way, you might say my depression symptoms blocked me from seeing the possibilities.

This reminds me of the classic story in which blind men gathered to experience an elephant.

"It's a pillar," said the blind man embracing one leg.

"No, a hand fan," said another holding an ear.

"You're wrong, a rope," said another.

"No, a wall."

"A solid pipe," said the one holding the tusk.

A wise man approached and explained, "You're all right. You all experienced a part of the elephant. The elephant is all that you said and more."

Finally, the blind men stopped arguing.

The same, I believe, is true about Deity. Everyone has a piece of the ALL. And what they don't see is that it is all connected. It's the same ALL that everyone else has. But they are experiencing the ALL in *different* ways, and this selective experience creates different practices and beliefs around the world.

So when I hear someone say that he knows the one and only God, I pause. I think of the elephant which is more than the sum of the parts.

Yes, I believe the God and Goddess are part of the ALL. But still I realize that Deity is more than my momentary perception.

I'd invite anyone else to consider that other people are experiencing Deity in a way that *suits them* at the moment.

Let's celebrate our shared opportunity to grow in spirit.

A WICCAN'S JOURNEY TO HEALTH

This section is a truly personal one for me. Being overweight most of my adult life, I accepted my size because it is a version of the Goddess.

Wiccans truly accept all body types. *This is good.*

For many of us, it is a relief *not* to have try to conform to the general culture's ideas of what is attractive.

I've noted that movie star bodies often require extremes of surgery, exercise and diet. That's not natural.

Our Wiccan culture values each person's natural body form as a representation of the God and Goddess.

Still, this is a hard section for me to write. In fact, I'm going to share something deeply personal, and I feel some dread.

I have come to a real crossroads of my life. First, I need to let you know that my mother is morbidly obese. And, she suffers from diabetes. She grunts in pain from simply walking around.

She has crossed from being "on the heavy side" to being **truly unhealthy**.

Having a healthy body is important for all of us Wiccans. When we have a healthy body, we can easily create energy to fuel our spells. But if we're unhealthy, we're often impaired and cannot raise the proper energy to manifest our desires.

If you can't walk up a flight of stairs, you sure aren't going to be able to dance and move to create energy properly. (Yes, there are other ways of raising energy. But why lose the joy of dancing and moving?)

Our bodies were meant to positively express themselves.

This is where I need to be truthful with myself. I am going to do something *no woman* I know wants to do: Admit her excess weight to the world.

I am currently 266.4 pounds. Let me put that into context. In high school, I weighed 113 pounds. In later years, I weighed 130 pounds, and I felt quite energetic at that weight.

My current weight of 266.4 pounds is aggravating my asthma. I feel out of breath after climbing a flight of stairs.

And I admit that I am scared to cross the line into diabetes. I know what suffering my mother endures!

My sweetheart supports me as best as he can. He goes for a long walk with me everyday. He bought me a treadmill when I alerted him to my difficulty breathing outside on a cold day.

So let's address this in few words.

- I agree with our Wiccan community in accepting all kinds of body shapes. Well done, community!
- I personally have crossed the line from "on the heavy side" to truly unhealthy.

In allowing myself to become unhealthy, I'm feeling bad in a number of ways: Pain in my hips, joints, back and more.

But there's something that bothers me just as much. I feel that I have let down the God and Goddess. They have given me this wonderful body as a temple, and in a way I've trashed it.

I do not want to disrespect the God and Goddess.

We're *not* talking about appearance at this moment. **We're talking about healthy or not healthy.**

So this is my call to action. I need to shed the excess weight and become what the Gods intended, to be a healthy version of me.

I have been taking action. On a number of days, I've walked 8,000 to 10,000 steps. That has resulted in my letting go of 10 pounds so far!

A good start.

I have written this section as both my personal declaration and as a support for any other Wiccans who, like me, want to cross the line *back to healthy*.

SKYCLAD VERSES ROBED WICCA

"Lisa, are you okay with going skyclad with our coven?" Sharon asked.

"I don't know," Lisa said.

"Do you understand why we go skyclad?"

"No."

It's your choice to go skyclad (which means nude) or clothed.

First, several covens do *not* practice going skyclad.

Some British Traditional Wiccan (BTW) covens do. For example, Gardnerians tend to, but many Gardnerian covens opt out of going skyclad.

Why go skyclad? Witches raise power. And, clothing is considered to insulate and prevent power from flowing.

Not everyone believes clothing has such a big impact. For example, I feel that magick is stronger than being so easily thwarted by clothing.

I note that we Wiccans try to attune ourselves as close to nature as possible. This is why most witches worship in the outdoors and honor the cycles of the seasons. Being in nature we feel closer to the Gods.

When we are born, we are naked, in a completely natural state. We are one with nature at that moment.

When we're skyclad, I feel, we're in a natural state. I feel this is a sign of freedom. We're free from society's chains.

For some, clothing ties into how lower social-economic groups are, in a sense, enslaved. Taking off those Reeboks and fancy clothes help witches to come together as equals in circle.

For a number of Gardnerians, going skyclad is a manifestation of tradition. *(Again, not all Gardnerian covens practice being skyclad.)*

For covens, who opt out of going skyclad, they use robes or even daily, casual clothing.

I suggest that you consider choosing some clothing that you keep *only* for ritual. Such clothing will help keep you in the ritual mindset.

Some covens choose to hold ritual in a backyard. And some neighbors would find seeing a group of skyclad Wiccans as "indecent."

Some people get a permit to hold a ritual in a public park (for example, the Spiral Dance in San Francisco, California). In these cases, going robed is a good idea.

Going robed works well when it's cold outside. You really can't concentrate if you're cold and uncomfortable. Honoring the Gods is supposed to be a pleasant experience after all!

Your robe gives you a cool opportunity: You can place all kinds of magickal symbols on your robe.

You can add the following to your robe:
- your name in Theban
- power sigils
- the color of your patron Deity
- herbs
- crystals (you could sew a few into your robe)

In this way, you can create magick just by putting on your robe.

Where can I get a Wiccan robe? There are sources on the Internet and at pagan gatherings.

If you feel crafty, you can even make your own. Consider this pattern below.

Front View

You can sew the robe together according to the marks on the above image.

Side View

When you make your robe, pick cotton or another natural fiber.

Remember, it's *your choice:* skyclad, robed, or in specially chosen casual clothes.

KEEP THE CONNECTION

My muscles ache and I'm wobbly on my feet. My Dad and I walk on a wooded trail in Pinecrest, California. My only thought is: *Can I make it to the car?*

On the drive back to our campsite, I think, *I really need to go hiking more often. My muscles are just not in the condition I'd like them to be in.*

Without enough hiking I lose valuable muscle mass and tone. And, without enough vigorous exercise, I'll lose bone mass or even get a "flabby" heart, a cause of other health problems.

How does this connect with Wicca? We see something similar: without enough practice, you can lose your competency in the Wiccan path. Just as muscles become weaker due to lack of use, so does your proficiency in Wicca.

Out of practice in Wicca, your spells will not be as effective. They can even go bad because you're failing to channel your energy to your desired goal. Such errors can cause undesired effects.

Fail to practice your faith and you may separate from nature which Wiccans hold so sacred. If you don't pay attention to the cycles of nature (the cycles of life and the seasons), you may lose compassion for others who are going through personal cycles of growth and sometimes personal pain. Human beings live in a cycle of puberty, aging and other personal challenges.

Separating from nature, you may even lose compassion for yourself.

On the other hand, you can be diligent in your practice. You can exercise your "Wiccan muscles" just as you would support your body through physical exercise.

When your Wiccan muscles are in tune, you'll take good care of yourself and stay aware of the Three Times Law (the reality that what you put out returns with three times the effect).

Be good to your spirit like you're good to your body through exercise.

Keep a diligent practice. Then you can avoid many situations of unintentionally hurting someone else. Through diligent practice, you are stronger and calmer. You have more patience.

So let's flex all of our muscles to be both spiritually and physically healthy.

Ideally, we put the effort into maintaining our health *and* into learning our lessons along the way . . .

WHERE IS THE WICCAN WISDOM?

Nina bit her lip. I could tell she was angry.

"Edna's not wise; she's just older!" Nina said.

It can work the other way. Have you ever met a young person with an *old soul?*

What about someone with a title? Does that make a big difference?

This is on my mind because I was talking with a friend who asked about my accomplishing the third degree as a Gardnerian priestess. Yes, I've studied for years with fine mentors. I've put in many hours and much effort into earning the third degree designation.

It's a strange thing about human beings. We expect certain things. Some of us expect that people would put effort into becoming wiser as they aged. Still, we've seen people who just seem to stop in their maturity level.

We expect, or at least hope, that someone with an advanced degree would show superior knowledge.

My mentors whom I've admired have demonstrated two traits: kindness and humility.

"The more I learn, the more I realize how much I don't know."
– Albert Einstein

Wicca, to me, is a life-long journey in which I learn new

things every week.

Recently, I wrote a section of this book about the 4 elements of the Witches Pyramid—which also includes Spirit.

The great thing about meditating in the Wiccan way is that often we are given insights from the Gods and Goddesses.

In essence, the more often you meditate, the more opportunities you have to receive guidance from the Gods and Goddesses.

One of my favorite insights given to me is *I am loved.* This gave me higher self-esteem, and this gave me an understanding that I was *not* a horrible person which was a faulty idea that depression had slammed upon me.

I invite you to keep meditating or to start a meditation practice. Open the door to a better understanding of yourself and the world around you.

EXPERIENCE FREEDOM THROUGH THE POWER OF FORGIVING YOURSELF

"You need to forgive yourself," my new therapist says. *Nice words,* I think. *How am I supposed to do that?*

I have been through many hours of therapy. I've experienced hours of meditation.

Here I'm going to talk about the truth and the reality of *Forgiving Yourself.*

Why do you need to forgive yourself?

Because feeling guilty and blaming yourself forms a damn prison. I know this prison well. At times, I have been mad at myself for somehow allowing others to harm me. How can you hold a 8-year-old little girl responsible for being held underwater by her sadistic 11 year old brother?!

Still, in later years, I had an abusive husband who had a hold on me until Wicca saved my life.

I've been furious with myself for "being a victim." I've said, "I know it is not my fault." But deep down I still felt it was my fault. I let it happen. I gave certain people power over me. I did this.

Whenever I go to this dark place, my heart bleeds tears of sorrow.

All of this self-blame and failing to forgive ourselves comprise a crime we are committing against ourselves.

Before I go further, I need to make something clear. Forgiveness is **not pardon**. A behavior could have been mean and negative two years ago, and it is still wrong today.

I learned from Dr. Fred Luskin (co-founder of the *Stanford Forgiveness Project*) that **"Forgiveness is the end of the cycle of blame and suffering."**

It is time we stop and forgive ourselves for the things we did to ourselves. We may also need to forgive ourselves for what we may have allowed to happen to us.

I'll now share an exercise that I've found to be powerful.

Warning: This is exercise IS powerful. **Make sure you have someone to talk to afterwards** —*a loving friend whom you trust, a counselor or a trusted psychologist. You might just save this exercise for a time when you can do the exercise in the presence of a trusted helper.*

Version One:
Have a friend you trust and who loves you sit in front of you. Be close enough to see into his or her eyes.

Get comfortable. Light a candle and some incense. (Place

the incense to the side so you avoid the smoke obscuring your view of your friend.)

Set a timer for 5 minutes. Then for 5 minutes, look into each other's eyes and think about how much you care about the other person.

Do this several times over a month. It may take longer or less time. Your plan is to get to the point where you feel relaxed and accepted.

Version Two:

Sit in front of a mirror and get comfortable. Light a candle and some incense. (Place the incense to the side so you avoid the smoke obscuring your view of your own eyes.)

After setting a timer for 5 minutes, concentrate as you look into your own eyes in the mirror. Now you begin the process of forgiving yourself for all of your past mistakes that caused you to suffer . . .

Say:

- **I forgive you for _____ and anytime I failed at _____.**
- **I forgive you for _____ and the times I was wrong.**
- **I forgive you for _____ and the times I let things happen to you.**
- **I forgive you for _____ and the times I hurt others.**

Do this as many times as you need so you start to relax into your personal forgiveness of yourself.

During the week, if you start to feel fearful or frantic, you likely need another session of self-forgiveness.

(Some traditions refer to this process as "mirror work." Some people practice saying, "I love you" to themselves as they gaze in a mirror. Many report that it takes about a month of practice until they feel better and a degree of real healing.)

After any session of self-forgiveness, *eat something.* You've used up personal energy. It takes energy *to focus* during your self-forgiveness session.

And then make sure to *talk to someone* you trust.

This is a very powerful exercise. Remember there is divinity in you.

As you do this self-forgiveness exercise, you will likely feel the presence of God and Goddess. How will you know this? You'll experience a degree of peace that is new and different than your regular daily experience of life.

Remember, *you are loved* by the God and Goddess.

CHAPTER FOUR:
SECRET #4: GODDESS WILL AUGMENT YOUR MAGICK

Many of us are drawn to Wicca because our soul thirsts for expressing the divinity that waits within.

Just yesterday, my friend Alicia practiced a form of magic. She needed to get a new car. Just before she went to bed, Alicia focused on all that she wanted in her next car: a certain price, an unusual shade of blue and low mileage.

The next morning, Alicia received a phone call from a dealership. A car of that exact shade of blue had arrived "off the truck." Alicia went in and discovered that car was perfect in color, price and had only 9,000 miles. (By the way, 9 is a sacred number.)

Alicia had worked a form of magick.

Secret #4 is Goddess will Augment your Magick.

In this chapter, we'll explore how to make your magick more positive and powerful. We'll also learn to avoid the big mistakes that cause havoc or no response at all.

Let's step forward into our magickal world . . .

THE GODDESS WANTS YOU TO HAVE WHAT YOU WANT

"Your aunt died this morning," my father said, his face twisted in pain. "She wouldn't eat. She didn't want to live, anymore."

Why had she stopped wanting to live?

Maybe this section finds you at a really tough time. Life can really hurt. We can get stuck thinking about what we don't have.

Many Wiccans are drawn to magick because they want something to make their lives better. Perhaps, you're longing for something to change in your life. Wanting things is not a bad thing. The Goddess wants us to be happy, and working on ourselves to bring something new into our lives can help us feel fulfilled. Maybe you want to make space in your home for something new like a corner of a room dedicated to your knitting materials or something else.

The real question becomes: How can we feel good now?— even if our thoughts are stuck on what we don't have.

Pause for a moment.

What are the things you already have in your life that you are grateful for?

What do you have that you like? An iPod? A watch?

I'm grateful for this chair I'm sitting in. It's more comfortable than the previous one.

My friend, "Sarah" lives at a level below the poverty line. But I notice that she pays attention to what the Goddess has already given her. She's happier than another friend, "Grant" who you'd think, with his high income, would be happy.

I invite you to center your thinking (for a time) on "what I have" instead of just "what I don't have."

In the moment, you'll likely feel better. This is a good thing. Then, when you turn to the Goddess asking for something that you desire, you're in a better space to do effective magick.

Be grateful for what you have to get around, whether its a new car, old car or your feet!

Being grateful for the things we already have will help us realize how fortunate we are. In such a good state of being, it is easier to connect with wanting to live.

At the time I wrote this section, we celebrated Mabon, which is a harvest festival during which we're thankful for what the Goddess has given us.

Let's continue our grateful feelings each day.

WHITE MAGIC VERSUS BLACK MAGIC —REALLY?

"When you're using Black Magick, you're " the comparative religion student said, as he stared at me.

"Hey, she hasn't said anything about Black Magick," the college class instructor clarified.

I added that Wicca is a *positive* spiritual path. I emphasized: "There is no White Magick or Black Magick."

Further in the discussion, another student asked, "Black Magick is about doing something bad to someone else—right?"

Still, another student said, "But I thought White Magic is when you do something good for someone."

Stop. First, this is a "dualism way of thinking." This type of thinking dates back many centuries. For example, in

Zoroastrianism, the One Deity was said to have two manifestations: good–Spenta Mainyu and bad–Angra Mainyu.

Some comparative religion scholars suggest that this good/bad idea continued through Judaism and Christianity.

This dualism idea is *not* the Wiccan approach. Modern Wicca traces back its insights to pre-Zoroastrianism times.

In Wicca, magick is energy and a resource. Similar to water, it is neither good nor bad.

Here are two examples about water:

Lost and staggering in the desert, you're parched, dehydrated. And water saves your life.

OR

You're taking a wonderful cruise, but a rogue wave knocks you from the deck. You tread water until . . . you can't, and the sea takes another victim.

So is water good or evil? No. It just *is*.

Wiccans can use magick for good or *bane ("a source of harm or ruin"*—Merriam-Webster.com). The *practitioner's intention* takes the resource that is magick and turns it to good or ill. Magick is simply the natural energies around us. I'll say that Black Magick and White Magick are misnomers.

So does this mean that the *practitioners* can be either White Witches or Black Witches?

I suggest we drop these terms.

Still, we *all* have a light and a dark side.

My point is: Let's drop these labels Black and White. Instead, remember *The Wiccan Rede:* "These Eight words the Rede fulfill: 'An Ye Harm None, Do What Ye Will.'"

Yes, evil exists.

But if we stick to *The Wiccan Rede,* we can walk a positive and spiritual path.

HOW TO PICK THE BEST SPELL ELEMENTS FOR YOU

"Could you help me pull together a spell to increase my confidence?" Lisa asked me.

"I've seen a couple of spells in books. But I'm confused. Which version should I use? What elements would work better for me?" Lisa continued.

This points to an important principle of practicing Wicca. Spells in books might be helpful. But we need to observe the reality that spells in books were written by someone else, and they were not written for you specifically. So how do you make a spell that works and is truly right for you?

Start by looking at a list of possible elements or items to include and observe what feelings you have about each one. If you don't have any emotional connections to an element, you might do better by choosing something that inspires something deeper in you.

Let's look at this process closely. Here is an example spell.

Spell for Confidence
What you will need:
- 1 yellow candle
- Yellow magickal ink or yellow pen
- Virgin Parchment or paper

Incense:
- Powdered Buckthorn
- Dragons blood
- Myrrh

Here's how the process can go. Mena sees the yellow pen

and it reminds her of a yellow tee-shirt she wore as a child. She had spilled her lunch on it, and kids in the schoolyard cruelly teased her about it. So yellow is *not* a color that Mena would use for her confidence spell.

On the other hand, Judy gave an excellent presentation in front of class at night school, and she wore a blue sweater. She remembers how great she felt. So she chooses to use blue ink and a blue candle. She taps into the memories and feelings of her past to help fuel her spell.

Judy looks at the incense, Powdered Buckthorn. But she had no prior feelings connected with it. Then she remembers her Grandma baking cookies made with allspice. Her Grandma always had a big smile for Judy, and she attended Judy's basketball games. Judy felt supported. She knew that Grandma believed in her. So Judy switches from Buckthorn to allspice.

Don't fear about making little tweaks to your spells to make them yours. When you make those tweaks, your spell will be more effective in reaching your goals.

THE DOWN AND DIRTY ABOUT LOVE SPELLS

I really like this guy. Can you do a love spell for me? Wiccans are faced with this question a lot.

Love spells can be quite sticky. There's a right way and a wrong way to approach them.

The Wrong Way to Do a Love Spell

Janet really likes Mark. So she buys a book on love spells

from the local book store. She finds one she likes and performs the spell that night on Mark.

The next day she sees Mark. There's something different about him. Soon he asks Janet for a date. During the date Mark can't keep his eyes off Janet.

In the next days, Mark can't get enough of Janet. At first she quite enjoys the attention. He calls every night.

Then he follows her to the gym, grocery store, a movie theater. He shows up at her house unexpectedly, at all hours of the day and night.

Now, every time she sees Mark, Janet jumps, startled.

Janet wanted love; she now has fear.

Do you see what happened? Janet made her own stalker by casting a love spell *upon* him. Two terrible details arise when you impose a love spell on someone. First, it's unethical to mess with someone's free will. Second, one could create a pattern in which a stalker may become violent.

The Right Way to Cast a Love Spell

Ellen hasn't been on a date in quite a while. At an evening class she attends each week, she likes three guys, but she's not sure about them.

She wants to find the right fit and someone who truly loves her. So Ellen decides to do a love spell. Ellen first decides to make the love spell about herself—that is, she seeks to become more accepting of love. During her ritual, she writes down what she'd prefer to find in a mate. She asks the Gods to guide her and that special person to meet.

A few days later, a guy named Sam arrives at the evening class. Sam is meeting one of the other three guys who attend the evening class. Sam strikes up a conversation with Ellen.

Some days later, Sam asks Ellen out on a date. They really hit it off.

Do you see the difference?

Janet did a love spell *on* Mark; and such an imposition should never be done.

On the other hand, Ellen did a love spell to make *her* more accepting of love and to be able to see the one she was looking for. She also asked the Gods to help guide both her and her right match to find each other.

That's a big difference.

Love Spell

What you will need:
- Pink candle
- Rose Oil to dress the candle. (You can make Rose Oil by diluting rose essential oil into olive oil. Make sure it is the therapeutic grade essential oil.)
- Candle holder for pink candle
- Loadstone
- Table for the altar
- Candles and candleholders for the four directions in the colors that represent each (red for south, blue for west, green for north, yellow for east)
- Red candle for the God and a green candle for the Goddess. (These candle colors are preferable but not mandatory. You may also use white candles, which represent all colors.)
- Working candle to represent the element Fire
- Cup or chalice
- Athame
- Pentagram
- Sword. (If you don't have one, use an athame to

cast the Circle.)
- Incense
- Censer
- Dish of salt, preferably sea salt
- Bowl of water
- Bell or chime
- Altar cloth to keep wax and the other things off the table
- Wine or juice and some sort of cake
- Lighter
- Taper (Light the taper by using the working candle. Then use the taper to light the other candles.)

The Basic Circle Script

Note: This script is written for someone who is casting alone.

1) Knock *three* times on the altar. Ring the bell *three* times.

2) Use the lighter to ignite the working candle. Place the lighter down on the altar. (The other candles will be lit later when you use the taper.)

3) Light the charcoal (if you are using it) from the working candle. (The incense will be placed on the charcoal later.)

4) Take your athame and place its tip into the flame of the working candle. Say:

I exorcise* you o creature of fire. And I consecrate and bless you in the names of the Goddess and the God that you are pure and clean.

(*Note: When we speak of *exorcise* here, we are purifying

the item by driving out any negative energies.)

5) Trace a pentacle (a five-pointed star) in the air above the flame. Pick up the working candle and raise it up above you and imagine the Gods' energy filling the candle's flame. Place the candle back on the altar.

6) Take your athame and place its tip into the bowl of water. Say:

I exorcise you, o creature of water. And I consecrate and bless you in the names of the Goddess and the God that you are pure and clean.

7) Using the athame, trace a pentacle in the water. Pick up the bowl of water and raise it up above you and imagine your energy and the Gods' energy filling the water. Place the bowl back on the altar.

8) Take your athame and place its tip into the salt. Say:

I exorcise you, o creature of salt. And I consecrate and bless you in the names of the Goddess and the God that you are pure and clean.

9) Using the athame, trace a pentacle in the salt. Pick up the bowl of salt and raise it up above you and imagine your energy and the Gods' energy filling the salt. Place the salt bowl back on the altar.

10) Take your athame and place its tip into the incense. Say:

I exorcise you, o creature of Air. And I consecrate and bless you in the names of the Goddess and the God that you are pure and clean.

11) Using your athame, trace a pentacle in the air above the incense. Pick up the incense and raise it up above you and imagine your energy and the Gods' energy filling the incense. Place the incense on the lit charcoal.

12) Take your athame and scoop up a blade of the salt. (Or you could use your finger.) Place this pinch of salt into the water. Repeat this step two more times. Now, with the athame, mix the salt into the water and finish making consecrated water. With the athame, trace a pentagram over the bowl. Now, pick up the bowl of consecrated water and raise it up above you and imagine your energy and the Gods' energy filling it.

13) Take the consecrated water (the salt and water mixture) and dip your fingers into it. Dab some of it on your inner wrists and forehead. Say:

I bless myself with Earth and Water.

14) Take the censer filled with the burning incense and wave the smoke over you. Say:

I bless myself with Air and Fire.

15) Take the consecrated water and use your fingers to asperge (sprinkle with consecrated water) the Circle. Starting with north and moving clockwise, walk a complete circle around the perimeter, aspersing each corner as you go. When finished, place the bowl back on the altar.

16) Pick up the censer. Use your hand to wave the incense smoke around the Circle. Starting with north and moving clockwise, walk a complete circle around the perimeter, waving the smoke as you go. Be careful not to burn yourself

or anything else. When finished, place the censer back on the altar.

You have just cleansed the space and yourself. Now let's continue by Casting the Circle.

17) Take the athame. Envision energy being channeled from you and coming out the tip of your athame [You point the athame outward, away from you as you create the Circle.] Starting with north and moving clockwise, walk a complete circle around the perimeter. As you walk, say:

I conjure you, o Circle of Power, that you be a boundary between the seen mundane world and the spirit world, that you protect me and contain the magick that I shall raise within you! I consecrate and bless you in the names of the Goddess and the God. So mote it be!

18) Finish at the east quarter (direction).

Now it's time to "call the quarters." (This refers to the four directions.)

19) Pick up the athame and the taper from the altar. Light the taper from the working candle. Go and stand in the east corner of where your Circle boundary is. Starting with the East Candle, say:

I summon, stir, and call you up, o mighty ones of the East, element of Air. Come guard my circle and witness my rite.

20) Trace a pentacle in the air with your athame. Then light the quarter candle for East. Say:

Hail and welcome!

21) Move clockwise to the South Candle. Say:

I summon, stir, and call you up, o mighty ones of the

South, element of Fire. Come guard my Circle and witness my rite.

22) Trace a pentacle in the air with your athame. Then light the quarter candle for South. Say:

Hail and welcome!

23) Move clockwise to the West Candle. Say:

I summon, stir, and call you up, o mighty ones of the West, element of Water. Come guard my Circle and witness my rite.

24) Trace a pentacle in the air with your athame. Then light the quarter candle for West. Say:

Hail and welcome!

25) Move clockwise to the North Candle. Say:

I summon, stir, and call you up, o mighty ones of the North, element of Earth. Come guard my Circle and witness my rite.

26) Trace a pentacle in the air with your athame. Then light the quarter candle for North. Say:

Hail and welcome!

27) Return to the altar. Using the taper, light the Goddess Candle, saying:

Welcome, my Lady!

28) Using the taper, light the God Candle, saying:

Welcome, my Lord!

You have now completed Casting your Circle.

The Spell:
Take up the pink candle and sprinkle some of the blessed water on it and say:

You are cleansed by water and earth.

Next wave the pink candle over the burning incense and say:
I charge and consecrate you by fire and air.

Do the same process with the rose oil and the lodestone.
  Next take your now cleansed and consecrated pink candle and carve your name on it with the word *love.*
  Next dress the candle with the rose oil and say:

Little candle, I name you (your name) you now represent the love I attract to me.

Place the pink candle into the candle holder and place them on the pentagram. Put the lodestone at the base of the candle.
  Take the taper and light it from the Working Candle and light the pink candle saying:

I am love and love comes to me.

As the pink candle burns, sit and concentrate on the candle flame, seeing love flowing in the form of light. When the candle has burned half way down, take the candle and drop three drops of wax on the lodestone. Return the candle to its original place.

Continue to see the love radiating from the pink candle, and now also see the lodestone pulling love to you.

Watch the pink candle until it burns completely out. Carry the stone with you to help attract love to you.

Cakes and Wine Ceremony

After any ritual, it is important to replenish and ground your energy. Begin with wine or juice.

1) Take the cup from your altar and pour the wine or juice into it. Then take the athame and dip its tip into the wine or juice. Say:

As the athame is to the male, so the cup is to the female, and so joined bring union and harmony.

2) Pour some of your blessed wine or juice into the offering bowl or plate on your altar. Say:

To the Gods!

You can now partake of the beverage.

3) Take your athame and point it over the cakes. Say:

Blessed be these cakes that they bestow health, peace, joy, strength, and that fulfillment of love that is perpetual happiness.

4) Take one of the cakes (or just a piece) and place it in the offering bowl or plate. Say:

To the Gods!

You can now partake of the blessed cakes.

So, what do you do with the blessed offerings in the offering dishes? You certainly don't just throw it into the garbage! They are gifts to the Gods. Take them outside to your garden where you can leave it on the ground to help nourish the Earth.

If you do not have a garden at your home, you can take the offerings out into the woods and leave them there. Some Wiccans who live in the city set the blessed offering out on their porch for local animals to partake. Be sure to only leave biodegradable food. Avoid wrappers or containers that will not decompose.

Closing Circle

It is *truly* important to dismiss the energies you have called for your Circle. Be sure to take down the magick temple (the Circle) you erected. And certainly dismiss the quarters!

To close your Circle:

1) Take your athame and hold it up and stand facing the East. Say:

Hail mighty ones of the East, the element of Air. I thank you for guarding my Circle and witnessing my rite. May you depart to your fair and lovely realms. I bid you hail and farewell.

2) Trace a pentacle in the air with your athame.

3) Continuing, moving in a clockwise circle, stand facing the South. Say:

Hail mighty ones of the South, the element of Fire. I thank you for guarding my Circle and witnessing my rite. May you depart to your fair and lovely realms. I bid you hail and farewell!

4) Trace a pentacle in the air with your athame.

5) Moving clockwise around the circle, stand facing the West. Say:

Hail mighty ones of the West, the element of Water. I thank you for guarding my Circle and witnessing my rite. May you depart to your fair and lovely realms. I bid you hail and farewell!

6) Trace a pentacle in the air with your athame.

7) Moving clockwise around the circle, stand facing the North. Say:

Hail mighty ones of the North, the element of Earth. I thank you for guarding my Circle and witnessing my rite. May you depart to your fair and lovely realms. I bid you hail and farewell!

8) Trace a pentacle in the air with your athame.

9) Return again to face the East. While walking the boundary of the circle, say:

Fire seal the Circle round,
Let it fade beneath the ground,
Let all things be as they once were before.

The Circle is now no more,
Merry meet, merry part,
And merry meet again!
So mote it be!

In the section, I have shared with you the wrong way and the right way for doing a love spell. Take care in how you go about doing a love spell.

A proper love spell will build you up and attract the right match for you.

[If you're interested in prosperity spells and other spells, please see my books *The Hidden Children of the Goddess* and *Beyond the Law of Attraction to Real Magic: How You Can Remove Blocks to Prosperity, Happiness and Inner Peace.*]

THE WITCHES PYRAMID—EARTH

"My life's just too busy. I'm juggling everything. Trying to keep my husband happy and our two children. Work is getting worse, too," Nadine told me.

"It sounds like you need a little 'silence' in your life," I suggested.

"Don't I wish!" Nadine confirmed.

In this section, I'm talking about the element Earth, represented as North of the Witches Pyramid.

The strength known as *to Remain Silent* is manifested as Earth.

Many of us find our thoughts racing all day long. It would really help if we could calm down our minds. As Wiccans, we find that quieting our minds helps us focus our thoughts and our magick. When you bring your mind to quiet, you can focus and manifest your desire into reality.

Furthermore, when we talk about *to Remain Silent,* we actually refer to *literally* being silent. For example, we stay silent about what happens when we conduct ritual. Everything done and said in Circle is sacred. This means that we Wiccans keep the details locked in our hearts and away from the mundane world.

Sure you might be tempted to share details of life-transforming occurrences in Circle. *Instead, be sure that you keep silent!* Keep the details as a precious, sweet experience all your own.

So how do you bring the element Earth and *to remain silent* into your life?

A Meditation to Celebrate Sacred Silence in Your Life

Find a quiet place where you will be alone and relaxed for five or ten minutes. Close your eyes. Breathe deeply. Picture a pyramid in your mind. Gently explore your answers to these questions:

What is this pyramid made out of?

What color is it?

What is the texture of your pyramid?

Imagine viewing the pyramid from various angles. Focus. Concentrate until you can even see the pyramid with your eyes open.

This pyramid process helps you focus your mind and clear it of extraneous thoughts.

Repeat this practice whenever you feel overwhelmed. Practice focusing, calming down and experiencing Sacred Silence.

More feelings of calm and peace are just a brief pyramid-meditation session away.

THE WITCHES PYRAMID – WATER

Karina turned to me and said, "But I've never done this before. It's a lot of money. I mean, I could spend all this money recording my songs and no one buys them."

"What does your heart say?" I replied. Sometimes, and it depends on the individual, the heart says, "It's time *to Dare.*"

The element Water represents *to Dare,* and Water is West on the Witches Pyramid.

Wanting to change isn't enough, we need more energy associated to the process. We need *to Dare* to do it!

Many of us are too afraid of change. We hide from it and even run from it. Still, we notice:

"There is nothing permanent except change." – Heraclitus

Change can be a very emotional subject. Being afraid of change is natural and so we need Water, to Dare ourselves to do it.

Change promotes growth. We grow not only spiritually, but also with our relationships and our mental and physical health.

A Ritual to Celebrate Water and to Move Beyond Fear

Consider something in your own life that you know you need to change but are afraid to.

Draw a pleasant, hot bath. Make a sachet of lavender. (For more about making a sachet, please see my book *The Hidden Children of the Goddess.* Lavender is used for purification, and lavender helps us calm those fears of change.

When your bath of lavender is ready, step in and relax. Breathe in and out slowly.

Once you have relaxed, think of the change you want and the fear holding you back from it. Concentrate on these fears you have.

Now envision the fear being absorbed by the water all while you continue breathing deeply—in and out.

When you feel you have successfully transferred all the fear into the liquid, get out and drain the water away. Dry off and make sure you do **not** use the towel again until you have laundered it.

Use this ritual focusing on Water and to Dare to move forward in your life.

THE WITCHES PYRAMID – AIR

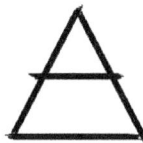

"Why is the Witches Pyramid important?" Sharon asked me. "You already told me that the pentagram emphasizes the four elements Air, Fire, Water, and Earth. Isn't that enough?"

I explained that the Witches Pyramid demonstrates how the four elements *support* Spirit.

First, I'll give you an overview. Here is how each Element relates to a direction and a concept:

Air – East – To know

Fire – South – To will

Water – West – To dare

Earth – North – To remain silent

These concepts come together to form an essential part of your Wiccan Practice.

In this section, we'll focus on Air.

Air – East – To know

Air is the cerebral element. You've probably heard the phrase: Knowledge is power.

In the Craft, we take action to *know* how to use the tools and rituals. Here is what is really powerful: to *know yourself*.

The journey of knowing yourself requires that you focus and take efforts to remove distractions. People who are caught up with their ego will miss so much.

Meditation provides a helpful path to discovering the truth that is deep within you.

How does meditation facilitate your self-knowledge? First, it helps you quiet your mind. Clear of distractions, you can learn about what you really need. Not just what you ego wants in this moment.

Clear of distractions, you can make better and better decisions. You'll have access to your intuition. You'll quiet down fear.

Clear of distractions, you'll connect better with the God and Goddess. You'll ask for guidance and you'll be able to take in and understand the guidance that arrives as intuitive ideas and nudges in certain positive directions.

Start Easy with Meditation

Many of us hear about meditation and freeze up. We may say, "I don't have the time." Start easy. Just set up a timer and meditate for five minutes. Simply find a quiet place. Get comfortable. Make sure you sit up so you don't fall asleep. Concentrate on your breathing. When your mind wanders, bring it back to your breathing.

You might even begin a practice with your romantic partner. My sweetheart and I sit near each other—not touching—and close our eyes for our five minute meditation practice. The good news is that when one of us is not in the mood to meditate, the other one can inspire the other one to sit for the five vital minutes of the day.

Certainly, you can expand your meditation time, if you like.

Some people get disappointed that they do not get a wonderful feeling when meditating. Know this: It all counts. With a regular practice of meditation, you make yourself calm and more receptive to guidance from the God and Goddess.

Meditation is a blessing for your mind.

Remember, your mind is your most important tool. And Air will assist you in your goals. This week, consider having a few meditation sessions in which you focus on Air.

THE WITCHES PYRAMID – FIRE

"I feel stuck," my friend Amy said. My first thought was that it might help for her to do a ritual related to the element Fire.

Fire, related to *South*, is an element that's part of the foundation of the Witches Pyramid.

Fire represents *To Will* on the Witches Pyramid. Will is that fire to get things done. Will is the *intensified-desire* that creates change and allows us to manifest our thoughts into reality.

Fire is energy. And still, we begin with the element Air which creates *the idea* of what you desire. Fire helps manifest what Air created.

Without Fire things stagnate. Nothing gets done. We need *to Will* to change ourselves and forge forward to accomplish the fulfillment of our needs.

Fire is a transformative element. Fire is a force (or energy) to change, which transforms you into something new

Change is something we strive for in Wicca. We want to transform ourselves into newer and better states of being so we can grow spiritually.

So how do we enhance the element of Fire in our lives?

Consider something you want to change or to get better in your life. Do you want to get a better job or do you need a better living situation? A quiet desire is *not* enough. You need to apply Fire so you **Will** something into being.

One of the best ways to empower yourself with **Will** is to do a ritual focused on Fire. Begin a meditation on Fire by first lighting a candle. Focus your eyes on the flame. Breathe deep. Soon you will close your eyes and do the following visualization.

Your visualization will now be quite *specific.* Visualize a symbol of a *current situation that you do NOT like.* Now imagine that what you really want is inside the symbol.

Now apply the power of Fire to the symbol which is like a false shell around what you want.

This false shell *burns away* and you are left with what you really want!

You have applied the power of Fire.

To build up your *To Will* power, you may need to do a series of Fire-related meditations.

Remember, your mind, properly harnessed, has terrific power to improve your life.

WITCHES PYRAMID – SPIRIT

"Why is Spirit included with the Elements that make up the Witches Pyramid?" Juliet asked.

"Spirit refers to your higher self and the Gods and Goddesses," I began. "The elements are the base of the Witches Pyramid. You need the elements plus Spirit to create life and to work magick."

The preferable order of the Elements is Earth, Water, Air and Fire. They incrementally increase in energy.

We begin with Earth since it is the grounding Element. As you work up with the higher and higher energy levels till you reach Fire, you use Earth to ground them all.

After working with Earth, Water, Air and Fire, it's natural to move to Spirit. When working with Spirit, we connect with our inner selves and the Gods. During meditation, you can receive messages and insights. We Wiccans strive to connect with Deity through nature, rituals and meditation sessions.

Wiccans work with Spirit in many ways that even connect with astral projection, psychometry (touching objects to sense them), and clairvoyance/clairaudience.

An Example of Connecting With the Gods

We know that life can be really tough to endure. Some time ago, I shared a particular chant (on my blog GoddessHasYourBack.com) to help you connect with the Gods and receive support.

Here is the chant you can recite to yourself when you're hurting:

By the Sun and by the Moon,
Let the Gods' light be my boon.
Shining deep and shining far,
May I be healed by every star.
I saw it then, I see it now,
Darkness be gone right here, right now!

You can use this short chant whenever you are feeling low. For example you can use this chant during meditation, lighting a candle or as a prelude to a meditation.

In discussing the Spirit aspect of the Witches Pyramid, we have completed our conversation of the components of the Witches Pyramid: Earth, Water, Air, Fire and Spirit.

We Wiccans can deepen our practice by repeatedly focusing on meditations related to the Elements.

FIND VALUE IN AND NUMEROLOGY AND ASTROLOGY

Recently, I've received questions about numerology and the Tarot coming through my blog GoddessHasYourBack.com.

So I'll start with overview provided by this below excerpt from my book *The Hidden Children of the Goddess*

* * *

"It's All About the Numbers

This section discusses the meaning of the numbers on the Tarot cards. We will also delve a bit into numerology.

People often ask about the "suits" of the cards.

Here are brief descriptions of the suits:

- Cup = water/emotion
- Pentacle = earth/wealth
- Wands = air/thought
- Swords = fire/energy that you use

The above four suits are considered "the minor arcana." Some authors suggest that the minor arcana are those things in life that you *can* change. On the other hand, certain authors emphasize that the "major arcana" are the essential strokes in life which are set.

Cards Ace (One) through King

Each Tarot card has a defined meaning, and each meaning relates to the suit it is in:

- Ace: represents the meaning of the suit and magnifies the lesson
- Two: balance, tension, or equilibrium of the suit
- Three: your spiritual path, mastery
- Four: for change, going through activity to rest and/or joy to discontentment
- Five: the negative side or attributes of the suit
- Six: lessons learned and actions taken
- Seven: decisions, facing a choice
- Eight: a difficult challenge
- Nine: a revelation
- Ten: the logical conclusion
- Page/Jack: the learning principle of the suit / what you can learn
- Knight: the active principle of the suit / enforces rules
- Queen: the reflective principle, a nurturing role; the queen guides you
- King: the ruling principle; the king has a dominant role, he makes the rules

Additionally the face cards of the Tarot can represent people in your life.

Let's return to the subject I mentioned: the major arcana.

The Major Arcana

0. The Fool
1. The Magician
2. The High Priestess
3. The Empress
4. The Emperor
5. The Hierophant
6. The Lovers
7. The Chariot
8. Strength
9. The Hermit
10. Wheel of Fortune
11. Justice
12. The Hanged Man
13. Death
14. Temperance
15. The Devil
16. The Tower
17. The Star
18. The Moon
19. The Sun
20. Judgment
21. The World

There is some controversy about how to approach the major arcana. Some people like to look up and strictly adhere to definitions that they find that describe each of the 22 cards of the major arcana. I have a somewhat different approach that allows *one's intuition* to play a significant role. For example, when you view the Chariot, you could look up the definition which often includes details like "strength," "combined power," and "moving forward."

At times, in the middle of reading a spread of Tarot Cards

for someone, I have interpreted the Chariot card as "travel, usually physically traveling."

So you can see Tarot card reading can be a highly interpretative and individualized process.

Timing and Numbers

Each card represents a specific number of days, weeks, or months that something will happen. The card's number is read together with its suit. (See below.)

- Cards Ace through Ten: 1 through 10 days, weeks, or months. For instance, a 5 of Swords means something will happen in about 5 days. An Ace of Pentacles means something will happen in about one month to one year.
- Page/Jack: 11 days, 11 weeks, or 11 months.
- Queen and King: unknown time (you're the factor for the time)

Suits and Timing

Each suit represents a different time frame.

- Swords: days (something will happen fast)
- Wands: days to weeks
- Cups: weeks to months
- Pentacles: months to years (something will happen slowly)

Numerology and How to Find the Theme of Your Year

The following equation will determine your theme for the current year. To provide an example, I will use a sample birth date for this year.

Month: 09

Day: 08

Current year: 2013

Now add together each number:

9 + 8 + 2013 = 2030

Now add together each number in the total:

2 + 0 + 3 + 0 = 5

Use the numbers on the Major Arcana to get your theme for the current year. You'll notice that for example, the theme is the Hierophant. A hierophant is someone who interprets sacred mysteries or arcane knowledge. So in this situation, one possible interpretation of the theme for the year is: One may face mysterious or religious challenges or changes.

0. The Fool
22. The Magician
23. The High Priestess
24. The Empress
25. The Emperor
26. The Hierophant
27. The Lovers

28. The Chariot
29. Strength
30. The Hermit
31. Wheel of Fortune
32. Justice
33. The Hanged Man
34. Death
35. Temperance
36. The Devil
37. The Tower
38. The Star
39. The Moon
40. The Sun
41. Judgment
42. The World

A similar formula will show your life path. Many Wiccans look upon the life path as the journey and goal of your time on this planet.

This time, use your birth date. Use the same list above to get your theme, that is, the central theme of your life path. For example "Kim's" birthday is September 7, 1993.

Month: 09

Day: 07

Birth year: 1993

Now add together each number:

9 + 7 + 1993 = 2009

Now add together each number in the total:

2 + 0 + 0 + 9 = 11

Kim's life path is Justice. One possible interpretation of this life path is that she may face a situation dealing with legal matters in her lifetime.

About Astrology

When people think of astrology, they often talk about the Sun Signs which form the twelve signs of the Zodiac. They are, in order, Aries, Taurus, Gemini, Cancer, Leo, Virgo, Libra, Scorpio, Sagittarius, Capricorn, Aquarius and Pisces.

Recently, at my blog, GoddessHasYourBack.com, I received this question: "I'm wondering about the astrological cusp of Sagittarius and Capricorn."

A cusp is when your Sun Sign is within three to five degrees either before of after the change in astrological (zodiac) signs.

The person who was born on the cusp of Sagittarius and Capricorn would have some traits of both the signs of Sagittarius and Capricorn. But the main influence would be the sign under which they were actually born.

In brief, here are some of the related traits:

Sagittarius: This person is said to have two personalities because the Centaur (Sagittarius symbol), is half horse and half person.

- The horse: rebellious, free-roaming, aggressive, gets bored easily
- The person: open-minded, honest, philosophical, clever.

It's suggested that these two personalities oppose each other every day.

Capricorn: The symbol for this sign is the Goat. Traits include: determined, conservative, helpful, and practical. A number of Capricorns are ambitious—not all.

Some people find it helpful to honor certain traits they find in their astrological signs. One friend is a Taurus which is noted as "stubborn and musical." So she makes sure to make time to compose some music every week. And she's stubborn about getting that time!

I invite you to consider the value found in elements of astrology and numerology.

HONORING THE GODS, CASTING CIRCLE, AND MORE

"I don't want to make a mistake. I'm new to spellwork," Claudia said.

Shifting the phone to my other ear, I thought, "I can empathize with this because I went through it, too."

Years ago, when I first began with Wicca, I was really concerned about doing Wicca correctly from the start. It was very important for me to honor the God and Goddess appropriately.

Claudia asked, "How do I do a dedication ceremony? It seems like there are a lot of ways to do it, depending on what kind of Traditions [Trads] are out there."

"It's true that there are many different types of dedication ceremonies," I began. "Many have valuable parts and there's no one and only way to do a dedication ceremony."

Wicca includes various rituals that a practitioner may do. Rituals can be incredibly complex to quite simple depending on your tastes. Do you like complex and complicated or do you prefer the more simple types of rituals? The best thing that I can say is whatever you do, do it from your heart. That is what pleases the Gods.

I continued by sharing my own journey and how I chose one of the oldest Trads for learning the basics.

Consider viewing the book, *Which Witch is Which?*, to get an overview of the different Trads out there.

Claudia then asked about the Casting of a Circle and why people enter from the East and leave from the West. I answered, "We start in the East, in the direction of the sunrise. Then you walk around deosil (clockwise or sun-wise) until you end up back in the East. West is the direction of Death so you exit that way. When you make a circle starting in the East, it comes around to the East again, making a 'door.'"

Think of the cycle of life and death. We are born just like the sun each day. And then the wheel turns until we end up at death, when the sun goes down or "dies."

Then Claudia asked about which colors are appropriate to use for your circle. You can use white. Or you can use colors that correspond to the four directions:

North – green or brown
South – red
East – yellow
West – blue

If you want more information, I have lots of good info for

beginners in my book *The Hidden Children of the Goddess*. My blog GoddessHasYourBack.com includes the article "Why Do Wiccans Do Ritual?"

"How do I find a good mentor?" Claudia asked and I shared with her information found in my blog post: *Finding the Right Wiccan Mentor for You.*

Another way to find a mentor is attending PantheaCon, a Pagan conference that takes place in the San Francisco Bay Area each February. Many different practitioners of Paganism (including Wicca) attend. You can then check out and ask about the different Trads, and learn from the practitioners themselves. You can check out the website of PantheaCon. It would be fun to talk with you if we meet there. I often attend.

You can also find local mentors through Covenant of the Goddess (website: cog.org).

I hope you find the above resources to be useful.

DISCOVER THE DEEP TRUTH
BENEATH CASTING CIRCLE AND RITUAL

I just couldn't get my mind to settle down. My friend's suicide happened and it really tore at my heart. I knew that I had to make sure that he transitioned safely to the Summerlands. The transition just wasn't going to happen on its own. That's what the Tarot told me.

So I pushed myself and took action. I did a ritual to help him find the Summerlands. Once I knew he had crossed safely, I felt peace in my heart.

For Wiccans, we do have a source of relief and even deep peace: Ritual.

In my studies, I've learned that Ritual is designed to get us *free* of the conscious mind and its petty obsessions.

The more often that you Cast a Circle, Conduct Ritual, Do the Cakes and Wine Ceremony and Close the Circle, you become *stronger*.

You become conditioned to go to a Higher Level where you can open the unconscious mind and open the doors to successful magick.

Successful magick happens when you open those doors wide and do it reliably. Repetition of rituals is the best way to change your consciousness so you can do magick reliably.

The more often you do ritual, the more you train your mind to make a transition to a Higher Level.

Each ritual begins with Casting a Circle. When you cast a Circle you not only set up your sacred space with related protection, your casting also opens those doors to your subconscious mind, which is called the Younger Self. We Wiccans use the Younger Self for communication as we do magick. By the way, the Younger Self is also known as the Sticky Self in the faerie tradition.

You might think of your Younger Self as a five-year-old. How do you keep a five-year-old engaged? Not with long-winded talking. Instead, you use things like props and other items. Think shiny, sparkly with loud noises.

Using drums, other musical instruments and other props that are fun and novel help you easily communicate with the Younger Self.

Wiccans realize the Younger Self is the source of energy for effectively doing magick.

Remember that regularly doing ritual helps you condition yourself to readily rise to a Higher Level and engage your Younger Self. In this way, your magick-work will get better.

THOUGHTS WE THINK AND THE MAGICK THEY CREATE: THE GOOD, THE BANE, THE MAGICKAL

What have you been thinking about today? Have you paused for a moment and listened to the words you say to yourself?

We know that words have power. The words we say can create change of emotion, of how we are treated—and even change the world.

What kind of words do you say to yourself—as a habit?

Do your words include:

- Good effort. You're getting closer to what you want.
- That's okay. You've learned something. You'll do better next time.

Recently, a friend pointed out that some of my words were really *unkind to me.*

I then realized that I've had the habit of saying certain mean things to myself:

- I can't do this.
- I just made myself look like a f—ing idiot.
- I can't do anything right.

Wow—it hurts just to write that down!

Words are connected to our habitual thoughts. Many of us don't really pay attention to what we tell ourselves on a daily basis.

As Wiccans, we need to pay attention to what we say because our thoughts and words hold power. If you repeat thoughts enough times, they become your reality. How is this true?

Let's look at one of the self-defeating thoughts I was telling myself: "I can't do this."

When I was younger, I wanted to be a writer. But my dyslexia kicked my butt. I told myself, "I keep getting it wrong so I must be a f—ing idiot so I can't do this."

I didn't come back to writing for 24 years!

So we see that your thoughts can actually cripple you. Your thoughts can kill your innate gift.

Don't let that happen. Become aware of your habitual thoughts.

Thoughts have their own magickal power. They can work for you or against you. They are a type of energy *and they manifest your view of reality.*

If you notice you are not feeling that great about yourself, ask these questions:

- What have I told myself lately?
- What have I been thinking about?
- Is it positive or negative?

Thoughts become beliefs if repeated often. This can be dangerous because these thoughts can manifest in our lives.

If you see negative things manifesting in your life, look at what you're telling yourself—because the thoughts are being sent out, and create what you see and how you see it.

We can replace negative thoughts with positive ones to create our own magickal transformation.

If you notice that you're putting yourself down, tell yourself, "Stop! Reframe." One of my own coaches brought this "Stop! Reframe" technique to my attention. The idea is to break the pattern and then "reframe" the situation by telling yourself something positive. In essence, you're giving yourself a new way to perceive the situation.

This process works for many people.

Additionally, I came up with my *own* process. If I think something negative, I tell myself, "Stop! *Goddess thought.*"

For example, sometimes, I put too much hot sauce on the eggs I prepare for my sweetheart. (Yes, he likes hot sauce on eggs. Go figure.)

I'll say, "Damn it. That was dumb!"

Then I'll tell myself, "Stop! *Goddess thought.*" I then *step out of myself* into the loving, compassionate energy of the Goddess. I then imagine what compassionate thing Goddess would tell me: "He'll be glad to get these eggs. You just saved him time and he was able to do more writing this morning. He always says something nice about receiving food that you make for him."

My point is that we, Wiccans, need to become our own best friend. Be the cheerleader of your own life. Remember our thoughts are always with us, just like the Gods. If you have trouble, ask the Gods for help. Look with Their eyes of compassion and *love for you.*

If you catch yourself making a cutting remark, say, "Stop! **Goddess Thought.**" Then look upon yourself with the loving eyes of the Goddess. Imagine what She would say to you to lift you up and bless you.

Doing this, you can change your view and your life.

DO NOT TURN YOUR MAGICK INTO A DISASTER

In several news broadcasts, TV anchors stressed the damage to crops and related water shortages caused by a severe drought. Angela could stand it no longer. She had to act! Angela cast a rain spell. Soon rain fell from the sky and the parched land soaked up the moisture. Then more rain and more. Mudslides caused property damage and even a few deaths.

Horrified, Angela realized that she had neglected to add a vital part to her rain spell—a timetable. She had *not* specified that the rain stop after the land was revitalized.

Destruction and death had occurred when Angela had *only* wanted to help the forests and farms.

Weather magick is quite tricky. You must ask for what you need and at the same time make sure there is a "stop-time" for the weather change you asked for.

The following is a little chant you can use to help the land, but at the same time stop the rain when you request it.

Rain Chant
Rain, rain come our way,
we ask you now to come this day!
Rain, rain come and play,
feed our crops now, in every way.
Rain, rain you've had your fun,
now go your way and give us sun.

Just like any spellwork, you need to tell the magick what to do and when its mission is complete. If you fail to do this, the results can be disastrous like Angela's experience.

Here's a way I can illustrate my point. You've probably seen the portion of Disney's *Fantasia* entitled "The Sorcerer's Apprentice." In the cartoon, Mickey enchants a broom to do one of his chores—filling a water basin in his mentor's home. Soon through Mickey's magical mistakes, the one broom became an army of brooms over filling the basin, creating a tidal wave of water.

Mickey had not used magick properly by guiding the

brooms to complete the work and avoid causing havoc. Lucky for Mickey, his mentor woke up and stopped the brooms' onslaught of water.

Many of us may *not* have a mentor to save us from ourselves. This is why it is a good idea to think through our actions before we do magick.

Let's think through our magickal plans and include "stop-orders" so we can avoid disaster.

Then we can simply enjoy the blessings.

HOW TO MAKE YOUR SPELLS MORE SUCCESSFUL

"What am I doing wrong in my spell-work? My spells are failing, even backfiring!" my friend, Jennifer, said, anguish in her voice.

As part of our conversation, I gave her some tips from my book *The Hidden Children of the Goddess.*

"You need several things to do successful magick.

1) Intent
To do successful magick, you need to understand several things. First, you must have an intent. You need to know what you want to manifest. Having a solid intent is your first step before you do any magick.

2) Concentration
This is the process of focusing and then refocusing your mind on your visualization task. In essence, you concentrate on the object and on the images in your mind that are specific for your desired manifestation

3) Visualization

You need to see what you want in your mind as already accomplished.

4) Willpower

The Collins English Dictionary defines *willpower* as "the ability to control oneself and determine one's actions." When it comes to successfully performing magick, willpower, to me, means the driving force of desire for some form of change. So I focus on the power of "I will." This is an important distinction because many people think of willpower as only the ability to avoid temptation."

[The above is the end of an abbreviated excerpt from my book, *The Hidden Children of the Goddess.*]

Check the Moon Phase

Is the moon phase helping or hindering your spell? Maybe your spell needs to be reworded to help it work more effectively. Take care to be quite specific in your wording.

Pick the Right Day of the Week

Different days are associated with different Deities and purposes, so choose a day that will lend energy to your spell.

Day	Solar Correspondence	Color	Magickal Correspondence	Deity
Mon	Moon	Silver, white and blue	illusion, prophetic dreaming, emotions, travel, and fertility	Diana
Tues	Mars	red, black & orange	courage & strength	Tyr, Tiu or Mars
Wed	Mercury	purple or orange	communication, change, cunning, and the arts, protection	Wodan (Odin) or Mercury
Thur	Jupiter	Blue	strength & abundance	Thor
Fri	Venus	aqua, pink	fertility, love, birth, and romance	Venus or Frigg
Sat	Saturn	Orange, purple, deep blue	material success, expansion, money/wealth, physical well-being, prosperity, leadership, and generosity	Saturn
Sun	The Sun	gold or yellow	personal achievements, success, wealth, fame, promotion at your job, seeking fame and wealth, or being acknowl-edged for a job well done	Helios

Magick is Like Water

Magick is like water that flows the easiest way down the mountain. Vague wording diverts your spell to an easy and wrong path. Be careful about your wording.

Be sure to follow the steps above and continue studying.

The Gods want to help you get what you want.

Do your part and get your spell-work in good shape.

MAKE MORE POWERFUL SPELLS

One night Sara did a prosperity spell. Feeling confident in her spellwork, she waited for the results of the spell to take effect. Three days later she *lost* her income source. What went wrong?

Doing spellwork is truly *work.* And, fortunately, you can improve your spellwork skills. Use the simple processes below to improve your success rate.

Moon Phase

Many Wiccans make a big mistake of failing to look at the moon phase before doing a spell. Because Sara didn't look at the moon when she did her prosperity spell, she missed the vital detail that the moon was waning. That's a problem because the waning moon is for decreasing work. She did *not* want her income to decrease!

What could Sara have done to have *more money* in her purse? She could have done a spell to *decrease* the size of her bills.

The truth is: You can do many spells at any time *if you word the spell correctly.*

As many Wiccans know, the waxing moon is for increase so it would have been better if Sara waited for the waxing moon if she wanted to stay with the original form of her prosperity spell.

Days of the Week

Another strategy for making your spell more potent is to use the correct day of the week. Plan to do your spell on the day that *rules* what you are seeking to accomplish. Here is an abbreviated list of the days, Deities and what they rule.

Sunday – Helios – Prosperity, power, strength, vitality, honor, passion

Monday – Diana – Agriculture, childbirth, instinct, a woman's cycles, secrets

Tuesday – Mars – Conflict resolution, drive, war, domination, justice, protection

Wednesday – Mercury – intellect, communication, mind and intellectual pursuits, law and court cases

Thursday – Jupiter – Travel, wisdom, animals, gambling, increase

Friday – Venus – Love spells, feminine issues, emotions, marriage

Saturday – Saturn – Discipline, responsibility, hard work

Planetary Hours

The next thing you can do to power up your spell is perform your spell at the correct hour.

Planetary Hours of the Day							
Hour	Sunday	Monday	Tuesday	Wednesday	Thursday	Friday	Saturday
1	Sun	Moon	Mars	Mercury	Jupiter	Venus	Saturn
2	Venus	Saturn	Sun	Moon	Mars	Mercury	Jupiter
3	Mercury	Jupiter	Venus	Saturn	Sun	Moon	Mars
4	Moon	Mars	Mercury	Jupiter	Venus	Saturn	Sun
5	Saturn	Sun	Moon	Mars	Mercury	Jupiter	Venus
6	Jupiter	Venus	Saturn	Sun	Moon	Mars	Mercury
7	Mars	Mercury	Jupiter	Venus	Saturn	Sun	Moon
8	Sun	Moon	Mars	Mercury	Jupiter	Venus	Saturn
9	Venus	Saturn	Sun	Moon	Mars	Mercury	Jupiter
10	Mercury	Jupiter	Venus	Saturn	Sun	Moon	Mars
11	Moon	Mars	Mercury	Jupiter	Venus	Saturn	Venus
12	Saturn	Sun	Moon	Mars	Mercury	Jupiter	Mercury

Planetary Hours of the Night							
Hour	Sunday	Monday	Tuesday	Wednesday	Thursday	Friday	Saturday
1	Jupiter	Venus	Saturn	Sun	Moon	Mars	Mercury
2	Mars	Mercury	Jupiter	Venus	Saturn	Sun	Moon
3	Sun	Moon	Mars	Mercury	Jupiter	Venus	Saturn
4	Venus	Saturn	Sun	Moon	Mars	Mercury	Jupiter
5	Mercury	Jupiter	Venus	Saturn	Sun	Moon	Mars
6	Moon	Mars	Mercury	Jupiter	Venus	Saturn	Sun
7	Saturn	Sun	Moon	Mars	Mercury	Jupiter	Venus
8	Jupiter	Venus	Saturn	Sun	Moon	Mars	Mercury
9	Mars	Mercury	Jupiter	Venus	Saturn	Sun	Moon
10	Sun	Moon	Mars	Mercury	Jupiter	Venus	Saturn
11	Venus	Saturn	Sun	Moon	Mars	Mercury	Jupiter
12	Mercury	Jupiter	Venus	Saturn	Sun	Moon	Mars

Supercharge your spellwork by adding the correct moon phase, day and planetary hour. Using these strategies adds energy to your spell. Such energy helps your intention, through your spellwork, find its mark.

CHAPTER FIVE:
SECRET #5: GODDESS INVITES YOU
TO LEARN SELF-PROTECTION

"How do Wiccans protect themselves?" Kristen asked.

"That's a big topic. What do you want to protect yourself from?" I asked.

"I recently graduated, and I'm temporarily living with my parents. They have a couple of friends who are negative. I want to keep my own room protected from their negative energy."

In this section, I'll share how to protect yourself by using salt.

[In the next few sections, I will share a number of ways to protect yourself. From House Blessings to guarding yourself from *energy vampires*, I've got you covered.]

We'll begin with one of the main techniques: using holy water. The Priest or Priestess takes sea salt and spring water and mixes them together. Then, the person blesses the mixture. A number of Wiccans say this: "I cast out all negative energies from this water, and I bless this pure water in the names of [pick which Deities]."

Then this mixture is used to cleanse spaces, objects and people.

Protection – Salt

Why do we use salt? Our ancestors noticed that adding salt to meat made it last much longer than if it was left alone. Although they didn't know it, the salt killed bacteria and germs so meat was kept edible.

But salt isn't just for a physical cleansing. Salt provides for a spiritual cleansing, too.

Bad energies and negative spirits don't like salt. So we use salt to cleanse the Circle we cast. We get rid of the nasties that may be lingering around. Think of salt as spiritual soap!

In the next section, we will talk about how Wiccans use the Circle for protection.

Protection – The Sacred Circle

Moira started her ritual. On the astral plane, this was like lighting a torch. Some entities were attracted. Fortunately, Moira's mentor taught her well; Moira made sure to **correctly cast** her Circle!

Among the reasons to cast a Circle, protection and raising energy are key.

Do you really need protection? Isn't nature all sacred? The short answer is . . . *yes*.

However, there are entities in the natural world that get attracted to a cast Circle. In the vastness of the astral plane, by casting a Circle, you have lighted a bright torch. The torch attracts everything. Entities are curious, and they're attracted to energy. It's what they feed on. So, in a way, you're ringing the dinner bell.

Casting a Circle and calling your quarters is how you defend your own energy and space. Casting a Circle creates a boundary that defends you from the little buggers on the astral plane.

When you call the quarters, you are summoning the elementals (a form of entity) that help you defend your Circle. They also donate power to your spiritual working.

Calling the quarters is part of building a fortress against unwanted entities that may try to interfere with you and the energy you are raising.

In essence, when you call the quarters, you are making a temple. A fortified and well-guarded temple.

Protection – Sage

"It's like she's still here!" Jennifer said.

"Who?" I asked.

"My mother-in-law. I don't know how Sam could come from that woman. When she's in the room with you, it's like being smothered in resentment and broken dreams."

"And you still feel her energy?" I asked.

"Yeah! How can it be? She finally went back to her home in New Jersey. But it's like I can't escape from her."

"Let me tell you about smudging," I said. Originally a Native American technique, smudging helps you cleanse a person or space for protection. Here's how smudging is a protection-technique. Negative energy sometimes gets on a person. Think of dog hair or cat hair. So you need to dispel this negative energy, and smudging does that.

Spiritual cleansing is a good way to protect yourself, just like washing your hands helps you stay healthy.

In smudging you use the sacred herb, sage. One process is to use a bundle of sage. You carefully light the end of the sage bundle, enough so that smoke rises from the end.

When you use sage it acts like a sponge that soaks up the negative energy of a place or a person (the person's aura).

How Burning Sage Connects with the Four Elements

Use an abalone shell as a holder for the sage bundle or loose leaves. The shell stands for the Element Water in the smudging process. The sage itself represents the Element Earth.

As the sage burns, we honor the Element Fire. The smoke rising from the burning sage represents the Element Air.

How to Use Sage to Cleanse a Space or a Person

You will need:
The bundle method: Gather enough of the herb sage to make a good pile of it. Use some cotton string or any other natural fiber and gather the sage. Bind the herb strands together to make a sage bundle.

Other method: You could place a pile of sage leaves in a fireproof container.

Next bless and consecrate your sage by using blessed holy water and incense from your altar.

When you are ready, light the sacred sage bundle and waft the smoke rising from the sage around the area to be cleansed.

As you waft the sacred sage smoke around the area, chant

or say an incantation of healing or clearing. Envision the sage smoke absorbing the negative energy of a space or a person's aura.

Fan the smoke and envision the negative energy dissolving away as the smoke dissipates. Make sure to open any windows and fan the smoke out of the home or away from the person being cleansed, healed and protected.

Protection – House Blessing

"What's wrong Jessica?" I asked

"We just finished moving into our new home," she said.

"How great!"

But Jessica's face told another story. "I don't feel like my family and I are the only ones there. Something just isn't right."

"Have you tried a house blessing?" I asked.

Sometimes moving into a new place doesn't bring the joy we had hoped for. We may experience a form of uneasiness.

Now, we'll discuss the process of doing a House Blessing.

What you will need:
- Large container of Kosher Sea Salt
- One white candle
- Spring or purified water (enough to asperge your entire home)
- Bowl (small)
- Bowl (large)
- Pitcher (this holds water for refilling your large bowl)
- Incense
- Anointing oil

- Athame
- White altar cloth
- Pentacle
- Bell

Set up your altar with the white candle (representing Fire) and the other Three Elements (Air, Water, and Earth). Put the white candle in the middle and the other Elements on their sides of the altar. Pour some water into the large bowl. Set the small bowl on the West side.

Section off the house with salt by making boundary lines blocking entryways for each room with the salt. (Set the salt in lines.) This will contain the energy in each room so that you can work on it as an individual space.

Start with blessing and purifying each Element by placing your athame in each Element—and say:

For the white candle: Light the candle, then place athame over it and say:

I CONSECRATE AND BLESS THIS FLAME IN THE NAMES OF THE GREAT LORD OF THE SUN AND GRACIOUS LADY OF THE MOON, THAT THIS FLAME BE THEIR SACRED LIGHT TO CAST OUT ALL DARKNESS WITH ITS USE.

Water Blessing:

I CONSECRATE AND BLESS THIS WATER IN THE NAMES OF THE GREAT LORD OF THE SUN AND THE GRACIOUS LADY ON THE MOON, THAT THIS WATER BE THEIR FERTILE ENERGY TO CREATE NEW BLESSINGS WITH ITS USE.

Salt Blessing:

I CONSECRATE AND BLESS THIS SALT IN THE NAMES OF THE GREAT LORD OF THE SUN AND THE GRACIOUS LADY ON THE MOON, THAT THIS SALT BE THEIR LOVING BODIES TO GROW NEW HOPE WITH ITS USE.

Incense Blessing:

I CONSECRATE AND BLESS THIS INCENSE IN THE NAMES OF THE GREAT LORD OF THE SUN AND THE GRACIOUS LADY ON THE MOON, THAT THIS INCENSE BE THEIR SACRED BREATH TO BREATHE NEW AND POSITIVE STORIES WITH ITS USE.

Take three pinches of salt and mix with the Blessed Water. Place incense on charcoal—or if using stick incense, light the incense-stick using the white candle.

Bless the oil with the Elements saying:

**I PURIFY WITH EARTH AND WATER.
I CLEANSE WITH FIRE AND AIR.**

Dip the small bowl into the large bowl to scoop up some Blessed Water.

Move around the space first with the water, asperge and say while going in deocil (clockwise):

I PURIFY YOU WITH EARTH AND WATER.

– Ring Bell

Next, move around the space while fanning the smoke of the burning incense and say:

I CLEANSE YOU WITH FIRE AND AIR.

– Ring Bell

If you sense any more negative energy, guide it with your hands. Direct the negative energy to the large bowl of holy water so that it is absorbed and cleansed. Shake the energy off your hands as you place your hands over the water bowl.

After purifying and cleansing the space, take up the athame and go to an entryway and trace a banishing pentagram there and say:

I CAST OUT ALL BANEFUL ENERGIES AND SEAL THIS [DOOR or WINDOW or FIREPLACE]

Then take up the oil and dab on each corner of the door frame/window/fireplace saying:

YOU ARE NOW CLOSED TO ALL NEGATIVE AND BANEFUL ENERGIES.

Once done, move to next room and start all over again.

When you have completed the ritual for the whole house, pour the last batch of the holy water down a sewage drain that goes *away* from the house.

This will help you clear all the nasties and bad energy from your home. You can also smudge your home afterwards just to make sure.

You deserve to enjoy your home in peace and harmony.

Protection – Shielding

"I feel so run down," Penny said.

"How are you sleeping?" I asked.

"Okay. But since I've started my new job, I've felt off. I even went to my doctor, and she couldn't find anything wrong with me."

"What is it about your job?"

"The work is good. I'm good at it. But sometimes I feel how certain people are so negative where I work."

"Have you tried shielding?" I asked.

Shielding can be done in many different ways. I will discuss two particular types here.

Casting a Circle is a type of shield.

Still, in this section we're discussing *personal shielding.*

One of my favorite exercises is to put up a shield (The Cosmic Egg Shield) during a specific form of meditation.

[Before I share the Tree of Life Meditation, I'll talk about "chakras."

Seven chakras are considered the most important, vital energy points on one's body.

Here is a brief overview:

The Seven Chakras
- Crown Chakra – "state of pure consciousness"
- Third-Eye Chakra – "relates to accessing intuition"
- Throat Chakra – "about communication and growth through expressing yourself"
- Heart Chakra – "relates to compassion, unconditional love, well-being"
- Solar Plexus Chakra – "relates to personal power, fear, anxiety, expansiveness"
- Sacral Chakra – "about basic emotional needs,

pleasure and even addictions"
- Root Chakra – "relates to the gonads, stability, and sensuality"

Now we will continue with the Tree of Life Meditation:

The Tree of Life Meditation/Cosmic Egg Shield

Meditation Exercise–"The Tree of Life"

Slowly breathe in and out. Breathe in the energy of love and peace (envision this as white energy). Breathe out all stress and negativity (envision this as black smoke). Keep taking deep breaths in and out. Concentrate on the white energy being breathed in and filling up your body with loving energy. Then let go and breathe out the negative energy you see as black smoke. As you do this, release the stresses of the day. Repeat this breathing cycle at least three times until you are comfortable and relaxed.

As your body and mind begin to relax, continue deep breathing and focus on this image:

Envision roots made up of energy sprout from the bottoms of your feet. With each breath, extend the roots farther and farther down toward Mother Earth.

Extend them down through the floor, down past the plumbing of the house, and down, down deep into Mother Earth's body. Go down to her core, to the center of her heart.

Once there, with each breath in, pull up the energy from Mother Earth. Breathe out the stress, and breathe in the blue-green energy of Mother Earth.

Pull the energy up through your roots, up past the plumbing of the house, past the floor, and into your feet. The energy feels clean and refreshing.

Breathe in deeply. Pull the blue-green energy up into your legs and past your knees. Pull it up, up into your Root Chakra at the base of your spine. Let it fill your body, going up, up into your Sacral Chakra and continuing to your Solar Plexus Chakra. Breathing in deeply, draw the energy up into your Heart Chakra. Let the energy flow down your arms and into your hands. Feel your body relax as the energy fills it.

Breathing in, draw the energy up into your Throat Chakra.

Concentrate on the blue-green energy filling your body. When you are ready, with another breath in, breathe the energy up into your Third-Eye Chakra.

Using your breath, draw the energy up into your Crown Chakra. Feel the energy flow throughout your body.

With another breath in, pull the energy up and out of your head. The energy forms like branches toward the Sky above you. Continue and let the branches flow up to the universe and out into the cosmos.

Draw down the golden energy of the Sky and universe into you. Continue to let the Sky energy intermingle and mix with the Earth energy that is already there. Pull it down through your body and into your arms.

Continue breathing deeply, mixing and pulling the energies down to your Heart Chakra.

Breathe in again, pulling the energy of the universe down into your Solar Plexus Chakra.

Continue pulling in the energy. Let it flow into you. Pull it into your Root Chakra. Breathing deeply, pull it down your legs and down to your feet.

Feel the energy from both the Earth Mother and the Sky Father that is within you.

Now focus on pulling this mixed energy out from the top of your head once more. But this time let it cascade down all around you like a waterfall until it completely surrounds you.

With a deep breath in, take the energy and push it out in all directions into an egg shape around you. This is the Cosmic Egg of Protection.

Keep breathing and as you do so, push out more and more energy into your egg.

Your egg gets stronger and stronger.

And when you are satisfied with the strength of your egg stop and relax.

In a moment or two, slowly start to pull your branches back within you, pulling them in with each breath.

Let any extra energy dissipate through the roots that you had placed into the Earth from your feet, keeping the egg intact.

Now breathe the roots up, and back into your body just like the branches that were above you. Give yourself over to the total relaxation you now feel.

In a moment or two—and when you are ready—open your eyes.

[Please know that you can record the above meditation and then listen to it later. Or you could invite a friend to read above script and guide you through the meditation.]

You have now made the Cosmic Egg Shield. This shield will protect you from absorbing negative energy. It will repel any baneful energy thrown at you.

Just remember to reinforce your egg.

The Second Form of Shield—The Cosmic Egg as Mirror Shield

Create the Cosmic Egg first as you learned with the process above. This time though, imagine the outer skin of the Cosmic Egg to be a mirror. This mirror will repel the energy thrown at you by energy vampires. Instead of being able to feed on your energy, the energy vampires' attempt will backfire, and the energy vampires will feed on themselves.

Caution: **Be careful about the powerful Cosmic Egg as Mirror Shield.** Wiccans are strongly guided to *harm none.* The Cosmic Egg as Mirror Shield is a "last resort" method to be used to defend yourself from someone trying purposely to harm you.

As I mentioned, the Mirror Shield will cause an energy vampire to feed on himself or herself. That is intense.

Please realize that some people do *not* mean you harm, they are just wired in a bad way. You don't want a friend or loved one to be harmed. It is wiser to use the regular Cosmic Egg process if you need to protect yourself from a non-malevolent energy vampire.

Be good to yourself.

Shield yourself in appropriate ways.

Protection – Talismans and Amulets

"Why do you wear that pentagram talisman, Moonwater?" my friend, Stephanie, asked.

"Protection," I replied.

"From what?" she asked.

Sometimes, I get surprised. In years past, I talked to her about how my brother terrorized me when he was 11 and I was 8. He held me underwater in a neighbor's swimming pool. I was sure that I would drown.

Later, Wicca helped me become strong enough to leave an abusive marriage.

So you'd think that she'd understand that I definitely want protection from *any* other tough things happening as I journey through life.

So I wear my pentagram talisman 24/7.

I feel that my talisman has protected me from near-collisions on freeways in Los Angeles. Also, the talisman heightened my awareness so I was able to avoid a speeding bus as I walked in San Francisco.

Amulets and Talismans—what's the difference? Amulets are found objects like four-leafed clovers. Talismans are man-made objects that are charged. You can make a talisman out of anything that's natural. Don't use man-made substances (plastic or otherwise).

How to Prepare Your Talisman

When you want to wear your protection, a talisman is ideal. You can make your talisman (that's the best). Or you could purchase one, and make sure you cleanse it of all energies before you start your ritual (see below).

Cleanse your talisman by placing it in a container of salt, making sure you have your talisman completely buried. Leave it buried under a full moon for three days. Say a simple chant like "I cleanse you of all energies, and I cleanse you under the silver moon."

Charging Your Talisman

First, be sure to charge your talisman **during the waxing moon.**

Cast Circle in the usual way.

Cense and Spurge the talisman. Dance to raise power while holding the talisman and place the energy into the talisman.

Now put the talisman on the pentagram of your altar and place your hands on top of both. Focus on the talisman and say this incantation:

I summon, stir and call you up, old and ancient powers of the Sun, Moon and Stars!

I summon, stir and call you up, old and ancient powers of the planets Mars, Venus and Jupiter!

I summon, stir and call you up, old and ancient powers of the planets Saturn, Mercury and Uranus!

I summon, stir and call you up, old and ancient powers of the North, South, East and West!

I summon, stir and call you up, old and ancient powers of the elements Earth, Air, Fire and Water!

I evoke you to place upon this talisman your strong powers of light and good, so that I may be protected always.

And that this talisman will work for good and will repel all ill luck and disasters away from me!

I _(your name)_ will this so! So mote it be!

Do the Cakes and Wine Ceremony.
Close your Circle in the usual fashion.

Consider bringing the power of a talisman into your life.

KEEPING THE HIDDEN CHILDREN HIDDEN

Nina is afraid. Did she leave her diary out on the kitchen table? Her deeply religious parents would disown her in a moment if they knew of her Wiccan path.

It makes sense that Nina keeps her spirituality to herself

at least until she upgrades to a better job and her own apartment.

Wiccans still suffer discrimination and intolerance in this world. It can even escalate to violence—bodily harm and damage to property.

We know *we* follow the God and Goddess, and we keep that a secret within our own hearts.

Realize that even if you are secure in being out as a Wiccan, many others are not. You do *not* know someone else's circumstances. You may live in a progressive location where you are safe. But others may live where they're *not* safe. Because of this, do **not** out anyone. Coming out as a Wiccan is solely a personal decision.

When you enter the world of Wicca and Paganism you need to abide by some rules which include:

- You keep the identities of the practitioners secret. Keep names, phone numbers and addresses both physical and email in confidence.
- All things said in Circle or Ceremony are sacred and secret.
- The *place* of meetings, called a *covenstead*, is kept secret.
- You do *not* touch any practitioner's tools without expressed consent of the owner of the tools.

Some Wiccans gather and go skyclad (naked) during rituals. This does NOT mean that there is an open invitation to touch.

The above rules remind us of ways to take care of ourselves and others.

WHAT MIGHT BE FADING FROM OUR WICCAN AND PAGAN COMMUNITY?

Two things recently shook me up. First, a friend told me about how a work group came to her house and then her camera was missing. This work group was made of pagans who participate in community events. What?!

Wicca, for example, is about respect for nature, respect for ourselves and respect for others. *What happened here that some pagan stole a camera?*

Second, two elders in our community told me about how they are being marginalized. "Younger Wiccans are not honoring elders. They don't listen," said one of the elders.

The above two incidents inspire the question: *Is our Wiccan and Pagan community letting an important part of our identity fade away?*

The part of our identity I'm talking about is being respectful. *Respect* is defined as "a feeling or understanding that someone or something is important, serious, etc., and should be treated in an appropriate way."

Elders and people's rights to their property need to be respected.

But there is something impinging on our Wiccan and Pagan community: For many of us, we're an island surrounded on all sides by the Western culture's self-centered ego, the "me, me, me" effect.

Have you noticed that if we get caught up in our thirst for instant gratification we lose touch with the roots of Wicca?

We're used to getting everything instantly. Through the internet, we have instant music, news, and contact with others. There is a casualty in all of this: patience.

And that's where the lack of respect for elders comes in.

Elders move and think at a different pace from those of us typing away at our electronic devices.

More than that, many of us think that elders are too behind the times to offer anything of value. What could elders teach us? Certainly, they can inform us of things to be careful about when doing ritual. Further, if they have had long-term friendships or a long-term romantic partnership, they know something valuable!

So how do we return to our Wiccan roots and enhance being respectful to others?

For many of us, we need to practice being respectful to the one person with us all the time—yourself. Show some patience and compassion toward yourself.

Then allow that patience and compassion to radiate out from you.

If you're going to be near an elder, pre-plan a couple of questions you might ask him or her.

Such questions might be:

- Knowing what you know now, what would you have done differently?
- You've been married 25 years. How did you do that?
- I hear that you've been friends with two people for 18 years. How did you take good care of your friends?

Elders have gone through life stages that many of us have not experienced yet. Sure, the details change. They may have used rotary dial phones, and we now have smart phones. But elders have gone through big and tough changes including loss of friends and loved ones to death, for example.

Wicca provides us with wisdom from the past. In fact, our Wiccan heritage has been passed down through the generations by *people talking to each other.* The process has usually been from elder to neophyte.

So I invite you see how you can make some space, pause and listen.

There's so much that elders can share with us.

BONUS CHAPTER:
HOW TO FIND A MENTOR
. . . AND MORE

THE IMPORTANCE OF MENTORING
AND THE EXPERIENECE

I placed the bowl of salt on the altar and then, gently, my mentor moved my hand to the left. Just then, I had the instinctive feeling that the bowl of salt was now in the right place.

I've found that having a mentor brings out an aspect of Wicca that one cannot find in a book.

Imagine trying to learn to swim without getting in the water.

Similarly, did you learn to ride a bicycle with no one next you? Learning to ride a bicycle is a good metaphor related to rising to higher levels of Wiccan practice.

You could read a book about a bicycle or watch other

people riding bicycles, but that is not the same as having a mentor guide you.

When my dad taught me to ride a bicycle, he was there offering advice and helping me right the bicycle when I took a couple of spills.

Wicca is an experiential process. A mentor can guide you in a progression of experiences so that you learn at a good pace and have successful experiences along the way.

The idea of being a mentor means so much to me that I'm now completing a video in which I talk directly with the viewer and show the process of a number of meditations. I provide guided meditations—this is a prime example of when a mentor can provide an experience to help the viewer go deeper in his or her practice.

Consider ways to bring a mentor or mentors into your journey.

You'll make progress faster and enjoy the journey more.

TRADITIONAL WICCA VERSUS "CYBER WICCA"

Have you wondered if practicing the old ways can really thrive in this fast-paced, high-tech age?

I think about this often. Walking my sacred path, I was fortunate to find a mentor and learn the sacred path in the traditional way, one on one. But what about those seekers who can't find a mentor to teach them the old ways face to face?

Wicca continues to grow in leaps and bounds. We're seeing that there are not enough mentors to go around with the growing demand for knowledge about our Craft. So many seekers turn to the Internet for help.

Is a Cyber Mentor going to work as well as an In-person Mentor?

The Pros and Cons When Comparing a Cyber Mentor and an In-person Mentor:

Cyber Mentor	
Pro	**Con**
Seeker can have access to the Cyber Mentor from anywhere in the world.	Mentor cannot see and feel how Seeker moves the energy.
Seeker has someone to go to for support.	Both Seeker and Mentor can only communicate through the Internet (or perhaps, occasionally by telephone).
Seeker may have a number of choices in terms of selecting an online mentor.	Mentor cannot experience how Seeker uses energy.
	Mentor cannot be present while the Seeker conducts ritual and provide in-person safety during the learning process.

In-person Mentor	
Pro	**Con**
Mentor is present and can give you an *experiential* understanding of Wicca.	Mentor may live far away, and meeting in-person may be quite difficult and time-consuming.
Mentor can physically sit with you and listen to your needs.	Mentor and Seeker may fall into personality clashes. Being present in-person may create an intense relationship.
Seeker has someone to go to for support.	Finding a compatible In-person Mentor may take much trial and error with related emotional ups and downs.
Mentor can read how Seeker processes energy.	
Mentor can lead you through meditations and can answer questions about the feelings that rise up during the process.	
Mentor can be there for Seeker's safety in learning the finer points of the Craft.	

Although, I prefer an In-person Mentor, I acknowledge that many Seekers are constrained by situations that require a Cyber Mentor. They may live in an area with no nearby mentors. They may have to hide while living where persecution makes it too dangerous to openly look for a mentor.

So Cyber Mentors come to be vital for many Wiccans' learning and training.

Through my blog, I function as a Cyber Mentor. I share my experiences in learning the sacred path. There are a number of good websites/mentors out there. It's often about finding someone who has a "voice" that really connects with your heart.

What would I suggest for those new to Wicca? Read to get insights from a number of credible people.

I have dyslexia so I've found that using an E-reader and enlarging the type help a lot.

You can start with these books listed here:

- *The Way of Four* by Deborah Lipp
- *When, Why....If* by Robin Wood
- *The Hidden Children of the Goddess: Embrace Wicca, Become Strong, Be at Peace with Yourself and the World Around You* by Moonwater SilverClaw
- *Goddess Has Your Back: How Wicca Can Help You Raise Your Self-Esteem and Make Your Life Magickal* by Moonwater SilverClaw
- *Beyond the Law of Attraction to Real Magick* by Moonwater SilverClaw
- *Buckland's Complete Book of Witchcraft* and *Witchcraft from the Inside* by Raymond Buckland
- *The God of the Witches* by Margaret Murray
- *Aradia* by Charles G. Leland
- *The White Goddess* by Robert Graves
- *The Golden Bough* by James George Frazer and Robert Fraser
- *Witchcraft Today, Meaning of Witchcraft* and a

suggested novel called: *High Magic's Aid* by Gerald Gardner

- *ABC's of Witchcraft* by Doreen Valiente
- *What Witches Do* and *The 8 Sabbats* by Janet & Stewart Ferrar
- *Grimoire of Shadows* by Ed Fitch
- *Robin Wood Tarot by The Book* by Robin Wood
- *The Sabbats* by Edain McCoy
- *The Circle Within* by Dianne Sylvan

Reading books like those above can help you on your first steps of your sacred Wiccan path.

FINDING THE RIGHT WICCAN MENTOR FOR YOU

The log of wood crackled as the campfire glowed. I stretched my feet, warming them near the fire, and I recalled a question raised by someone who commented on one of my blog posts. *She asked about how to find a good mentor.*

So I wanted to share with you the following *List to Help You Find a Good Mentor.*

If you're just beginning on your Wiccan path, you may experience the difficulty in finding the *right* Wiccan mentor *for you.*

The good news is: When you find the right mentor, magick happens!

So here are some essential questions to ask yourself as you seek *a great mentor for you.*

- **Are you safe?**

Safety is the most important detail here. If you don't feel safe or you don't trust the person who will be mentoring you, then it's likely a *bad situation*. Listen to both your mind and your intuition. Do *not* take unnecessary risks. Leave or avoid the person. Safety first.

- **Do you two get along well?**

The mentor-student relationship is a special one. Feeling good and connected to a mentor helps in the learning process.

- **Does the person abide by** *The Wiccan Rede?*

If the person does not live according to "An it harm none," you can*not* trust that he or she will be good to you, too. Hurting others is simply wrong. If you see that the person does things that mess with another person's will, *get away* from the potential Wiccan mentor.

- **Does the person align with the Law of Three?**

Does the potential Wiccan mentor understand and accept responsibility related to the repercussions of his or her actions? The Law of Three holds that you will receive three times what you put out into the world. People who do bad things attract three times the trouble *not only* to themselves but to others associated with them. Get away from those who do bad things!

- **Is this person compassionate and respectful?**

Some mentors are tyrants. A mentor who is a tyrant fails to demonstrate compassion and respect in many areas of life. If this potential mentor has no respect or compassion for others, ask yourself, "How will he/she ultimately treat me?"

Avoid this potential mentor.

● Does this person manipulate others?

Pay close attention. Do you see the possible mentor manipulating other people for selfish ends? It's a fallacy that this kind of mentor will treat you "as special." No! If the person hurts others, then at some point, such a person will hurt you, too! Avoid this type of mentor.

● Does this person come highly recommended?

A rule of thumb for working with someone new is to talk with three people who have had previous interactions with the person. Certainly, you would ask about the level of the potential mentor's knowledge. But even more important is to ask: "Would you work with this person again?" If the person does not have three people who unreservedly recommend him or her, then *beware*. So many people allow their desires to blind them to the truth. Do *not* let this happen to you. If you hear bad news about the person, heed it!

Use the above essential questions to help you find the right mentor for you.

Be safe by using both your mind and intuition.

MENTORING

I focused the video camera on the Golden Gate Bridge. I was filming some footage for my upcoming video program. After I got the shot, my friend turned to me and asked, "You mentioned that this video is to help people avoid mistakes when doing magick. What was a mistake that you did?"

This started me thinking. Actually, it was *the fear of making mistakes* that *prevented* me from doing a lot while I was a solitary practitioner. I avoided spell-work because I was *afraid* of doing something wrong.

A number of times, I could have asked for help from the Gods, but I was afraid of doing a full spell because I was not sure about all of the proper details of casting a Circle, conducting a ritual and closing the Circle.

In a way, I'm glad that I hesitated. One of the big mistakes that people make is improperly closing a Circle or not even closing a Circle.

I replied to my friend. "My big hope with my video program is to function like a mentor to the viewers. My own mentor has saved me from making a number of mistakes. And because of that, *I've done many rituals with confidence* that I was doing the proper tasks in the correct order."

As a mentor, I'm often asked to provide certain rituals to help a person navigate a transition. To commit the self to the path of Wicca, new practitioners often use a "Dedication Rite."

DEDICATION RITE

I have had many requests for help in writing dedication rituals. So here is a simple dedication ritual that you can do if you have made the choice that Wicca is right for you.

Dedication Rite Preparation

Turn your phone off and make sure you will not be disturbed. Clean the area to do ritual: Dust, vacuum, and anything else you need to do before you begin. Next take a ritual bath. Find a comfortable place and sit quietly, meditating on what you are about to do. You are about to dedicate yourself to the path of the Gods. Be honest. Is this really what you want to do? Don't take the promises lightly. You will also need to pick out a new name to go by. This is fun and can be anything you choose.

What you will need:

1) **Cakes/Bread:** It is acceptable to use bread, cupcakes, cookies, or even a power bar. It should contain carbohydrates to nourish the body and replenish the energy you use during the ritual.

2) **Censer & Incense:** In this case, the incense burner holds cone incense. However, it is acceptable to burn any kind of incense you choose. Remember that incense, when burned, represents Air on your altar.

3) **Taper:** The taper is for lighting candles. You begin by using a lighter to ignite the wick of the working candle. Then, you bring the taper to the working candle and ignite the wick of the taper. Now with the lit taper you ignite the other candles on your altar.

4) **Lighter:** The lighter is used to light the working candle. Any type of lighter may be used.

5) **Bell/Chime:** A bell or chime is needed for different purposes during a ritual.

6) **Pentacle:** The pentacle is used to help focus your attention on your goal.

7) **Athame:** The athame knife is used to direct power and can cast Circles.

8) **Bowl with Water:** Water is one of the five elements. It is used together with salt to make consecrated water.

9) **Dish with Salt:** Salt represents the Earth. It is placed into water to make consecrated water.

10) **Chalice with Wine:** As you remember, the cup is a female symbol. In a ritual, the cup holds the wine or juice that is to be blessed. (It is acceptable to use juice instead of wine if you do not drink alcohol.)

11) **Offering Dishes:** These dishes are used to "offer up," as an offering, part of your blessed food from your "cakes and wine" ceremony. We will discuss that later. You can also offer up flowers, which pay tribute to nature and the Goddess.

12) **Goddess Candle & God Candle:** These are the candles that represent the God and Goddess.

13) **Working Candle:** The working candle is positioned between the God and Goddess candle. Use this candle to light the other candles during a ritual. The working candle represents the element Fire on your altar.

1) Cast Circle
2) Dedication Rite

Say the following:

O Triumphant and Great Lord,

O Beautiful and Gracious Lady,

My intention to You, my Lord and Lady, is to dedicate myself onto the sacred path which you have opened before me. I accept this path as my own, and willingly of my own accord tread upon it. I know it will not be easy, but I promise I will be steadfast. And if I should fall, I shall rise again, all in Your honor. I will help those who tread upon the path, with me, beside me and behind me. And I will help them freely and willingly with love in my heart, for I know that they are a part of You as I am a part of You.

(Raise goblet or cup)

As I kneel before you naked in this truth. I [Your New Name] toast to you O Honorable Lord and Gracious Lady.

To new beginnings, new friendships and new growth.

Magick in the starlight
Magick in the moonlight
Magick is now my right.

So Mote it Be.

3) Do the Cakes and Wine Ceremony
4) Close the Circle

I hope this dedication rite will help you upon your journey.

YOUR PATH CONTINUES

As we complete this journey with this book, I celebrate your efforts and spiritual growth.

Please continue your journey with me by viewing my articles at my blog at GoddessHasYourBack.com

Additionally, learn rituals, chants, tips, and ways to customize your rituals just for you ... and even more when you sign up my exclusive enewsletters. Just go to GoddessHasYourBack.com and click on the link (on the right side of the webpage).

Blessed Be,
Moonwater SilverClaw

ABOUT THE AUTHOR

Moonwater SilverClaw is a Wiccan High Priestess and member of the Covenant of the Goddess and the New Wiccan Church. She has trained people new to Wicca. Her personal story reveals how Wicca saved her life and helped her strengthen herself to secure her release from an abusive marriage.

Moonwater has been practicing Wicca since 1990, first as a solitary and then in a coven.

Moonwater posts at her blog,

GoddessHasYourBack.com

[with visitors from 173 countries]

She felt called to write the blog even through she is dyslexic. She works with a team of editors. She says, "I wish to educate those who don't understand what the Craft is about. Some people may not yet identify themselves as pagan, but they'd like more information."

Moonwater has addressed college students in Comparative Religion classes for over ten years. She leads workshops. She lives with her cat Magick and her sweetheart of many years; he is one of her editors. She enjoys knitting and photography.

Her work is endorsed by Wiccan notables including Patrick McCollum (receiver of the Mahatma Gandhi Award for the Advancement of Religious Pluralism).

Moonwater SilverClaw can be contacted at:

AskAWitchNow@gmail.com

Or at her blog:

GoddessHasYourBack.com

Special Offer Just for Readers of this Book:
Contact Moonwater SilverClaw at askawitchnow@gmail.com for special discounts on books, coaching, workshops and presentations. Just mention your experience with this book.

EXCERPT FROM
GODDESS HAS YOUR BACK

by Moonwater SilverClaw

CHAPTER 1:
GODDESS HAS YOUR BACK

Would you like your Wiccan path to lift up your self-esteem?

Would you simply like to feel better?

This book helps you actually feel your connection with the Goddess on a daily basis—even moment to moment.

As I mentioned in my first two books, *The Hidden Children of the Goddess* and *Beyond the Law of Attraction to Real Magick,* Wicca saved my life and empowered me to leave an abusive marriage.

As a High Priestess, I have supported friends, family, and colleagues in times of need. My blog TheHiddenChildrenoftheGoddess.com gives me a weekly opportunity to support website visitors from over 173 countries.

This book gives *us* the space and time to really explore magickal practices, rituals, meditations and experiences that you'll find comforting and uplifting.

My journey upon this path began with meeting the Gods. The Gods showed me the true path to self love and acceptance. Where I saw nothingness and unworthiness, they showed me abundance and a unique specialness that I had.

Now I will let you in on a secret. *You have your own unique specialness that no one else has.* It is yours, and yours alone. This new path is yours to discover and walk. Just like my own path, your path is a beautiful discovery simply waiting for you. Prepare to step forward on this new, wondrous, and beautiful path.

Let's take the next step.

Secret of How to Do Magick

When I first started doing magick it was really hit or miss, most often *mess*. My spell work was just not as effective as I wanted it to be. What was I doing wrong?

If you have wondered the same thing, you have probably done similar mistakes. For example, I'd do a money spell, but I'd just get new problems!

The real problem was, like many people, I just wanted a big payday. What I didn't know was that this is really the wrong way to approach a lack of money.

Many, if not most, spells written today are focused on the external opportunities or even requesting gifts from the Gods. Focusing on just the external can create new problems.

What if I could tell you a **Secret of how to do magick**—in a way where you avoid ethics issues about money?

I have mentored a number of people about this *Secret*. Now I will share with you this Secret.

A phrase from the poem by Doreen Valiente entitled *The Charge of the Goddess* tells us how to do magick well. But many of us, like my younger self, just don't see it. The line I'm talking about is: "...if that which thou seekest thou findest not within thee, thou wilt never find it without thee."

This line invites us to look within as we approach our magickal work.

Instead of focusing on how to get money from outside sources, focus within. How? Instead of asking for a handout from the universe, ask, **"How I can create more energy in myself to obtain my desire? How can I make myself open to more prosperity?"**

Let's get more specific. You have been laid off and need a new job pronto! Bills are pilling up fast.

Let's use a sigil for this purpose.

How to Make Your Own Personal Sigils

Imagine putting a magical intention into an object. Why would you do that? Wiccans do this because they want the object to hold power to help them realize a personal desire. For example, you may be job hunting and you want the power of the object—in this case, a sigil—to assist you to get the ideal job.

Making your own personal sigils is easy. Some time ago, author/artist Austin Osman Spare devised a method for creating sigils.

Since that time, a number of authors have discussed Austin Osman Spare's process of making sigils. One book I appreciate is Frater U. D.'s *Practical Sigil Magic: Creating Personal Symbols for Success*.

I have made a couple of my own additions to the process.

First, throughout history, witches made sigils out of virgin parchment. But that is quite expensive. Also if you're vegan and will not wear leather, you will want to use something else. Why? Parchment is typically made from sheep skin. So let's talk about a process devoid of parchment.

I use the heavier art paper, the kind that absorbs ink and which can be infused with different tinctures made with herbs. Watercolor paper is a nice choice, too.

What about inks? You could use one of the many magickal inks on the market. My favorite is Dragons Blood Ink. But magickal inks can be expensive. So you can make your own out of a high grade ink such as Winsor Newton ink or India ink. To make it a magickal ink just add some essential oil to it, like myrrh. Mix and consecrate.

You can even use Sharpie pens as author Peter Paddon suggests. Just make sure to designate specific pens for only magickal work. They'll be part of your set of magickal tools.

You can use different colors for different desires. Here is a short list of colors and meanings that I include in my book *The Hidden Children of the Goddess:*

- Red: sex, desire, vitality, strength
- Orange: charm, confidence, joy, persuasion
- Yellow: intellectual development, joy, intellectual strength
- Green: prosperity, abundance, fertility, money matters
- Blue: healing, protection, spiritual development
- Purple: the occult, power, magick
- Pink: love, friendship, compassion
- White: purity, innocence, peace, tranquility

Write out your desire on a scratch piece of paper; you can use a single word or a phrase. Some examples are:

- I want an ideal job for me at this time

- Happiness
- I need a new house
- Success

We'll now use the word "Success" as our example. Cross off all of the repeat letters in Success. You end up with S, U, C, and E. (You want only one of each letter that appears in the word.) Next, scramble the letters, getting S, E, U, and C (for example).

Now comes the fun part: Combine the letters together in an image.

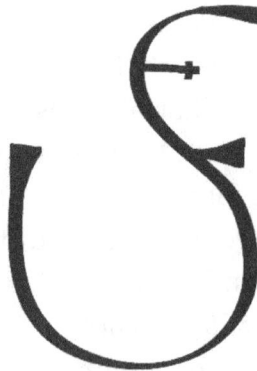

Success Sigil

Can you find the letters?

In this way you can make all sorts of sigils.

If you want to imbue it with a potion or tincture, this is the time to do it. You can either soak the paper in your tincture or brush it on. Either way you must let it dry. Overnight is best.

Now with this new image (of combined letters), inscribe it with your magical ink on your absorbent paper.

Now that you have the sigil, the next step is to breathe life into it with Pranic Breathing, also known as belly breathing. If you're familiar with yoga, you are probably familiar with

Pranic Breathing techniques. Breathe in deeply; allow your stomach to inflate. Visualize pulling up energy from the earth. When you have built up enough energy in your lungs, blow it onto the sigil. This will charge it with your energy and further empower your intention.

Now place your sigil in a safe place and forget about it. Forgetting about it is the toughest part of the whole process. This helps the magick work.

As you can see, making your own sigils is quite easy and fun. After some practice, you will be able to do them quickly and easily.

Remember the Gods are here to help. You can call on them for inner strength.

How to phrase a sentence for a sigil to get a job:

- All blocks I have put up, known and unknown, dissolve so that I am a good candidate and my future employer hires me.
- Help me express the inner strength, skills and energy so that I can acquire a job of my liking.

Here are phrases for those who have an interest in an entrepreneurial path:

- I find new ways to serve others successfully so that money comes to me naturally.
- All blocks I have put up, known and unknown, dissolve so that I can create abundance in my life.

Can you see how each sentence or phrase focuses on inner change, not the external "give me, give me"? With these phrases you are not looking for a handout. **You are creating the abundance by changing *yourself.***

This can be applied to the rest of your magick as well.

Another example is love spells. Focus your magick on *being more loving, or more open to love.* Never do love spells *upon* a particular person. Instead do a spell to attract love to you in whatever form is appropriate by creating yourself as more loving.

By focusing on inner change and developing our inner strengths, we can achieve our desires.

Goddess Has Your Back in the Worst Times

When you're reading a book what are you looking for? I'm looking for the truth and some way to become stronger. I promise to provide both for you in this chapter.

END OF EXCERPT
from *Goddess Has Your Back*
Available from Amazon.com

* * * * * *

Excerpt from *Beyond the Law of Attraction to Real Magic* by Moonwater SilverClaw

Beyond the Law of Attraction to Real Magick
How You Can Remove Blocks to Prosperity, Happiness and Inner Peace

Self-perspective: Overcome the Blockage of Not Feeling Worthy

Do you feel worthy of the best that life has to offer? Maybe on the conscious level you say, "Sure. Bring it on. The new house, new car, and a real, loving relationship."

But have you ever sabotaged your chances of getting exactly what you wanted?

Self-sabotage can occur because of feeling not worthy on a subconscious level.

If it's subconscious, how can we deal with this?

Good question.

Soon I will share with you a Self-Love meditation.

But first let's talk about magick. The whole premise of this book is that there is a way to go about the Law of Attraction with more power.

To put it simply, the Law of Attraction is a form of magick, but people who read an introductory book on the Law of Attraction are often denied enough information to truly make the Law of Attraction work in their own lives.

So to really make a positive difference in your life, we need to talk about real magick. I spell magick with a "k" to distinguish it from stage magic you see on television.

Magick is a natural power, *not* a supernatural one. Who uses magick? In my spiritual path, Wicca, one is trained to use magick in appropriate ways.

When Wiccans do magick, they channel *natural* energies and create change with them.

Well, if Wicca isn't really supernatural, then why practice Wicca at all?

To put it simply, *you want something.* That's probably why you were interested in the Law of Attraction in the first place. Now in the context of learning real magick, you'll be able to fully use the Law of Attraction. And that's good news!

Everyone is different and has their own answer to that question. I like to think of religion as a bottle of wine. Let's say you have three different people who all taste the same bottle of wine. The first person points out that the flavor has accents of oak. The second praises the hints of apple in it, and the third enjoys the floral notes. They are all right. The wine contains all the flavors they described. But each person detected something different. Religion is like that. Deity can't be entirely known. So the truth of it is scattered into many faiths.

In Wicca, we honor the God and the Goddess. If that's new to you, you can substitute the label of Higher Power or God or Deity.

The Gods and Goddesses have helped me and they can help you, too. The first thing they taught me was self-love.

Before we go further, let's make a distinction between self-love and self-conceit (or being stuck in one's ego).

Self-love is about kindness and support. So it's a good thing. It is NOT about your ego or puffing yourself up.

Let me show you how the Gods changed my perspective on myself for the better.

One of the best exercises I learned is meditation. Through reflective meditation, the Gods helped me understand how skewed my perception of myself really was. This was a key turning point for me.

One thing you always hear about are affirmations, but for many of us these just don't work.

First, let's cover what an affirmation is. It's a personal, positive statement. It can be as simple as "I feel terrific" or "I make a lot of money."

For many, the above statements don't work. Why?

A number of people have said, "It just sounds like I'm lying to myself."

Like myself, many people's inner self-beliefs interfere with these positive statements. For an example, if I used the affirmation "I am thin," my brain would object with "No,

I'm not. Look in the mirror." It's not true. No matter how hard you try to pound that new idea into your brain, your brain pounds just as hard back.

So how did the Gods help me deal with this problem? They inspired me to create a Self-Love Meditation.

So instead of the uphill battle of an affirmation, we'll use the Self-Love Meditation to work with the situation.

END OF EXCERPT
from *Beyond the Law of Attraction to Real Magick*

Purchase your copy of the above books (paperback or ebook) at
Amazon.com or BarnesandNoble.com
See **Free Chapters** of Moonwater SilverClaw's 4 books at http://amzn.to/1tni9WP